The Italian Campaign

One Soldier's Story of
a Forgotten War

Albert DeFazio

as told to

Valerie DeFazio Vacula

MERRIAM PRESS

HOOSICK FALLS, NEW YORK

2020

First published in 2015 by the Merriam Press

Third Edition (2020)

This work is a newly expanded edition of *The Italian Campaign: The Forgotten War* by Albert DeFazio as told to Valerie DeFazio Vacula, originally self-published by the authors in 2014, and republished by Merriam Press by arrangement with the authors.

ISBN 978-1-57638-513-5
Library of Congress Control Number 2015915553

This work was designed, produced, and published in
the United States of America by the

Merriam Press
489 South Street
Hoosick Falls NY 12090

E-mail: ray@merriam-press.com
Web site: merriam-press.com

Dedication

The 36th "Texas" Infantry Division, the 143rd Infantry Regiment, Company A, and all companies in the regiment who fought the campaign in Italy.

I would like to thank all veterans, past and present, who fought and continue to fight today for the freedom of this great country.

To Todd DePastino and the Veterans Breakfast Club, where veterans share their war stories after many years of trying to forget. I thank Todd for putting this club together. I feel being able to talk about the war has made a difference for many of us.

To my family, including my son Albert and especially my daughter Valerie, who made this book possible.

Contents

Foreword

I was a young teen when I found out my dad had been at war, but it wasn't until I was in my late forties that I learned, through his writings, about his time in the Italian campaign. I cried while reading his memoir and couldn't believe that my dad had seen and gone through all that he had. I thank God that He kept him safe and brought him home to his family. My dad endured the pain of shrapnel embedded in his back, a concussion, and years of nightmares. But all in all, he turned out to be a good husband and father.

When I was eleven years old I went to my dad and told him that I wanted to be a majorette and march in a drum and baton corps. Excited about my interest, he said we would talk to a friend of his who was the director of one of the top corps in our area. I told him I didn't want to be in that one because I didn't like the military-looking uniforms they wore. I preferred the uniforms of the other corps in our area because they were all frilly and cute. He said, "Well, how about we go to both of their rehearsals and see which we like better."

It turned out that my dad's friend wanted to put me in their color guard, but my dad told him I had my heart set on being a majorette, so we went to see the other corps. Although we were impressed with them, my dad had a different idea. He started his own drum and baton corps. That's when I learned that my dad had been a drummer himself and marched in the Vern Acklin Cavaliers after the war.

It didn't take him long to come up with a name, and soon the "Stars and Stripes" were born. We started out practicing in the basement of a local church, and our first parade was in Sharpsburg, Pennsylvania. Since we were still raising money for uniforms, we wore navy blue shorts, white blouses, and tennis shoes with red pom-poms. It took only a year before we had real uniforms and, although they were red, white and blue, they were not military-looking and I was happy with that.

The Stars and Stripes became an award-winning corps, winning trophies and prize money through the years. We even beat the two more established corps in our area. I could always tell by my dad's face whether we won or not. He would try to hide his excitement and may have fooled the other kids, but not me.

My dad was proud of his accomplishment and loved every one of the kids that marched in the corps. They truly loved him as well. They affectionately called him "Mr. D," a name that stuck with him for his entire life of the Stars and Stripes, and still today whenever he runs into a former member. There were times when a child had to leave the corps that they loved so much because of financial reasons. My dad would step in and tell the parents not to worry — the corps would pay their dues. But what people didn't know is that my dad actually paid for them out of his own pocket.

As a corps we had fundraisers that kept us running for twenty-seven years. We did hoagie sales and sold candy bars. Every Christmas we would make hard tack candy in the kitchen of our church. We would make two thousand pounds and sell every bag we made.

As the corps began to grow in size, we needed more space to practice, so we moved to the local elementary school and practiced indoors in the winter and in the parking lot outside in the summer. The drummers practiced in the hallway, majorettes in the gym, and the color guard in the cafeteria, which was separated only by a curtain and stage. It was loud but got even louder when, for the last half hour of practice, we were brought together and did our routine as a corps. My dad stood there every rehearsal inside that gym.

My dad missed only one parade in all those years, and we sometimes had two to three parades per week. He didn't ride in the equipment truck either — he walked alongside of us every step of the way. We not only marched in parades around Pittsburgh, but also traveled to other states and even Canada.

We were only a junior corps, so there was an age limit on who could participate. When I aged out, I became the majorette instructor and later taught the color guard. I was able to do both because I'd had years of private lessons in baton twirling, then later I marched in the Vern Acklin Cavaliers, the same corps my dad marched in as a drummer. Later I joined the Pittsburgh Rockets who years later became the Steel City Ambassadors. My brother Albert took after my dad and became a snare drummer.

Year after year the Stars and Stripes had a routine that was accompanied by a patriotic song, whether it was "Stars and Stripes Forever" or "You're a Grand Old Flag" or "National Emblem March." My dad never strayed from incorporating patriotic songs, though I never understood why it was so important to him.

After all those years in the corps, I read my dad's memoirs. It finally hit me why we were called Stars and Stripes and why we performed so many patriotic songs. He had fought for the freedom of his country, and, after all he had gone through, this country meant so much to him. Then I thought of all those loud practices in the gym and how he hid the fact that he had post-traumatic stress disorder and loud noises startled him easily. Of course we didn't know this at the time, but once I found out I could remember sometimes seeing something in his face that wasn't right. Nonetheless, our time in the corps was, I believe, the happiest time in my dad's life. It made him forget what he had gone through and got him out and about. Before that, he never liked to travel or go anywhere; he was happy simply being at home. He loved that corps as he loved his country. He may not like to take credit or to hear that he was a hero for what he did, but he'll always be my hero.

After hours of research and months of reading, I learned so much about the Italian campaign. I was shocked to realize that my dad had lived to tell about World War II, the largest, most violent armed conflict in the history of mankind.

Preface

One day I was in my bedroom cleaning out drawers when my then teenage daughter, Valerie, walked in. There was a medal lying on the bed, so she asked, "Dad, where did you get this medal? Did you win it?" I said, "Kind of." I started to tell her how I had gotten it while in the war.

"You were in the war? Which war?" she asked, a surprised look on her face.

My wife, who could be funny at times, said from the other room, "He was in the Civil War."

I explained to Valerie that it was a Purple Heart that I received in World War II when I was wounded. Valerie stood there for a moment staring at it and said, "I never knew you were in the war — where were you shot?" "In my back." I explained that a bomb had exploded not far from me and I was struck with shrapnel. "Well, did you ever kill anyone?" She asked as she looked at the medal.

I looked away. "I don't know. I hope not." It was a long time before we spoke of it again.

Years later I had gone to a picnic held for our local state representative, Tony DeLuca. While there, I had a chance to speak with Mr. DeLuca, and he told me about a gentleman that wanted to talk to World War II veterans. He gave his name and said he works for Congressman Mike Doyle. I went to see him, and he explained to me that there were two thousand World War II vets dying each day. The gentleman asked if I wouldn't mind writing my own story so it could be placed in their archives. I went home and thought about it for a few days. At the time I was in my late seventies. I was retired and had nothing else to do, so I sat down and started to handwrite my war story. I gave it to the gentleman to send in, he made a copy of it and handed me the original back. It sat in my drawer for years.

A couple of years ago a neighbor and good friend of mine, Bill Mansfield, took me to a veteran's breakfast where I met a young man named Todd DePastino. Todd is in charge of a club called

The Veteran's Breakfast Club, which hold a breakfast every couple months in different areas around Pittsburgh. This breakfast was in Penn Hills, which is where I live. The club draws many veterans — mostly from World War II, but any veteran can attend. One of these mornings I had a chance to sit down and tell Todd about my time in the war. He tried for months to get me to stand up and tell my story at breakfast, but I always turned him down. I would listen to other vets talk and listen to Todd talk about different battles of World War II. Never was the campaign in Italy talked about. Finally, at one breakfast I gave in and told Todd I would speak, which made him very happy. I'm not one for speaking in front of big crowds, but I did it so people would understand that the Italian campaign was just as important as the rest of the war.

When people speak of the war, the first things they think of are D-Day, storming the beaches at Normandy, war in the Pacific, or the Battle of the Bulge (where my older brother Pat had been injured with a bullet in the neck). You never hear about Monte Cassino and the Italian campaign — it's as if it has been forgotten. The Italian campaign involved some of the hardest fighting in the war and cost the United States forces some 114,000 casualties. The campaign played an important part in determining the eventual outcome of the war.

At the age of 89 I pulled my story from the drawer, and now I want to share it with all.

Chapter 1

Growing Up Italian

My mother and father were born in Altavilla, Italy, a small town outside of Naples. Although they only lived around the corner from each other, they never met until they came to America. My father, Antonio DeFazio was born May 17, 1883. When he left the port of Naples, he was nineteen years old; he arrived at Ellis Island on May 23, 1902. After landing at Ellis Island, my father spent some time in New York before he went to Boston, Massachusetts. There he worked in construction, only to have fallen from a building and have a beam land on him, breaking his leg, which left him with a limp for the rest of his life. He stayed there for a short period of time before leaving and settling in a small town outside of Pittsburgh, Pennsylvania, called Verona. He then got a job at Union Steel in Lawrenceville, but it was only a few days a week. Then the Depression hit in 1929 and everybody was out of work — I mean nobody was working. People then got on relief or welfare as it is known, getting whatever they could, food or some cash assistance. There were seven of us, so we got seven dollars a week.

My mother, Giuseppina Galasso, was born April 15, 1899. She also left from the Port of Naples and then arrived at Ellis Island on October 28, 1920, at age twenty-one. She went to live with her brother Benny in Philadelphia and worked in his store. A short time later my mother and her brother moved to Pittsburgh. They settled in the small town of Verona, and there my Uncle Benny introduced my parents to each other.

My parents had five children: four boys and a girl. My brothers Bill and Pat were the oldest and I was the middle child (born in 1925), followed by my sister Angie and my brother Anthony. We were all born in a one bedroom bungalow next to the railroad tracks in Verona. Later my father bought another house a few doors away. It was bigger, so we moved there but still owned the other house. In fact after we all started to work my mother told my oldest brother to call and find out how much we owed the government and pay it back. It wasn't much, a couple of thousand, but we had to pay it back because there was a lien on the house. My mother wanted to do right — after all she had appreciated the seven dollars a week. We grew up speaking Italian, we learned Italian before we learned English. We lived in an Italian neighborhood and that's all anyone spoke.

My dad made homemade wine as far back as I can remember. That's all my family drank — my dad would drink water sometimes just for the fun of it. It was 1936, the year of the big flood in Pittsburgh, and we were about to lose the house because of the water rushing in from all the rain. My father made sure we tied and anchored the wine barrels down so he didn't lose them. He didn't care about the house, just the wine. As kids we were allowed to have wine on Sundays, that's when everyone would come to our house and play cards and talk. Whoever won the hand of cards would then get to drink the wine and then they would give it to one paisan after another. It was good times. My mother would then serve salami, sopressata, homemade Italian bread or whatever we had. I can still smell that bread she made, my kids still talk about it today. I never ate store-bought bread, not until I left home. My daughter Valerie loved going there on Sundays as a child, she loved my mother's spaghetti sauce and bread.

We had a garden up on South Verona hill. We would come home from school and go work in the garden. Whatever we picked we'd haul it on our shoulders from South Verona hill down across the boulevard and home then sell it, corn was 15 cents a dozen. There were tomatoes, peppers, greens, any kind of vegetable you wanted, we had. What was left my mother would can. We may not have had money but we never went to bed hungry.

As kids we spent most of our time down by the river, we'd swim every day but never went alone and if we couldn't swim then we would be playing ball. We played mushball, baseball wasn't big at the time. It was like softball only the ball was bigger and softer.

We went to St. Joes School in Verona for a few years. Back then the school was an all-wooden building so we would go early in the morning and fire up the stoves for heat. No indoor bathrooms either, we had an outhouse. The nuns back then were tough, but they were good teachers. They kept you disciplined, they didn't have a problem smacking your hands with a ruler and they didn't care how bad it hurt. If you didn't learn from them it was your own fault.

My parents finally became American citizens. They had to learn English, and be able to read and write their own names. They really killed the English language but at least they learned it. My kids would laugh when they heard my mother and I talk because we would speak Italian then all of a sudden an English word or two would be said. Valerie and Albert had a tough time understanding my mother but they managed to pick up words here and there. Valerie was two years old when my pop died so she really didn't remember him. But he always called her Ballerina instead of Valerie because she always walked on her toes.

When I turned sixteen, I quit school and went to work for the Oakmont Water Authority as a flagman for thirty-five cents an hour. I did what I could to help my family, I mean we all did. When they laid me off I went to work for American Steel Foundries, but in less than a year I was drafted by the Army. My brother Pat had been drafted the year before me. My other two brothers enlisted after World War II was over.

I remember hearing the story of the Sullivan brothers who were from Waterloo, Iowa. They were five brothers who enlisted in the Navy with the stipulation that they serve together. At the time the Navy had a policy of separating siblings, but it wasn't strictly enforced. On November 13, 1942, the Sullivan brothers' ship, called the USS *Juneau*, was struck by a Japanese torpedo and sunk, instantly killing three of the brothers. One brother drowned the next day. Four or five days later, another suffering delirium and insanity with the grief of losing his brothers, decided to go over the side of his raft he occupied. He was never seen again. Knowing this story, I was glad at the time that my brothers and I did not serve together.

Chapter 2

Basic Training

I was eighteen and received my draft notice. I was told to go downtown and get my physical. Weeks later I was sent to the training grounds in Aberdeen, Maryland. It was there they interviewed me asking all kinds of questions. The interviewer asked, "Did you graduate?" I said, "No, I quit school at sixteen." He asked about my mother and father. I was also asked, since I was of Italian descent and might end up fighting in Italy, would I have a problem shooting at an Italian. I found it to be an odd question but understood it could happen since America was not yet allies with Italy. I answered, "If someone is shooting at me, I'm shooting back no matter who they are." Finally they ask what branch of the service do I want to serve in. I tell them I'd like to try the Marines and they replied no. "Well then the Navy," I said. "No." Then I was told, "We're going to put you in the Infantry because you don't have a high school education or diploma." "Why did you even ask me?" I asked. "We have to," he answered.

Later they sent me to the quartermasters where they gave us all our uniforms. Shoes, they just take a look at you and guess your size then tell you to put them on. I said, "Hey, these are too big." He said, "Well, exchange them wherever you go." I understood because all those men coming through, they couldn't take the time to measure.

I was shipped to Camp Shelby, Mississippi, and placed in the 69th Division that was one of the divisions in World War I, The Fighting 69th. I was then ready for my thirteen weeks of Army training. It was tough and rigorous, but it didn't hurt you. If anything it made you a man. At first they wanted to make me a bugle boy. They handed me a bugle and told me to report to the lieutenant in charge. I knew that I didn't want to be a bugle boy, so when I got there I told the lieutenant, "They handed me this thing and I have no idea what it is or what I'm supposed to do with it." He grabbed it from my hand and told me to go back to the base. That ended me becoming a bugle boy. Of course I knew what it was all along, I had no desire to play the bugle. Later we went on twenty mile hiking trips and exercised hard daily. Every muscle in my body ached and I could barely walk. As days passed, my body no longer hurt and training began to feel really good. I remember a guy in basic training who was a wise guy and hard to get along with. One day our staff sergeant, who happened to be an American Indian, had had enough of this wise guy. He took him out behind the latrine and beat the crap out of him. It straightened the guy out and he was never any trouble again.

When basic training was over, I was sent home for two weeks. Other than my family, there was no one else around because my friends had all been drafted like me. Before I knew it, two weeks had passed and I was glad to be back at Camp Shelby.

When I returned I was told that the paymaster had wanted to see me. I went to see him and he told me to sign the payroll book and take my $21.50 in cash for my monthly pay. I said, "I already got my pay." He said, "No, you were not paid." I said again that I was already paid. He said, "Sign the book and take your money and leave." So I did. Wouldn't you know it, one year later while I was in Italy, I received a letter from the paymaster's office. They had overpaid me in the amount of $21.50 and deducted it from my pay check. I guess there are times you just can't get anything over on the Army.

One day at Camp Shelby we were called together and they started reading names off a list. "These are the people going overseas," they announced. They called the list in alphabetical order, and my name was missing. When they were finished, they said there was another list called the "supernumerary list." I found out that my name was on that list. When they were done reading that list I asked, "What is this super list that you got me on?" "In case somebody on the first list cannot go, they'll pick someone from the super list," I was told.

That didn't sit well with me. I went to the company commander and told him, "I want to go overseas with my friends. I know these guys and trust them." The commander told me, "This came down from headquarters, and there's nothing I can do about it." I tried to plead my case, but nothing I said seemed to help. When I left he could tell how upset I was. The next day the lieutenant came to see me and said, "DeFazio, I don't know what you did or said, but you're on the list to go now." I would be shipping out with my friends and believe me I was elated.

Chapter 3

Shipping Out

When the day came, they shipped us to Newport News, Virginia, where they put us in a convoy of five hundred ships. There were submarine destroyers to protect us. There were five hundred men on a Liberty ship that was commanded by the Merchant Marines. It was really tight quarters — nose to nose in the bunks. We sat anchored all night waiting for the convoy to start out. Finally come morning they were ready to take off. We ran into a huge storm that nearly washed me overboard. It scared the hell out of me. I had no idea where we were headed. They nearly starved us to death — when they called us up for chow it was only round crackers and a drink. I was wanting more but there was nothing. I thought maybe later that evening they would give us something else, but again there was nothing. A day or two later someone broke into the ship's storage and found cases of K rations and C rations. They started to hand them up to the GIs. Later, people found out we had been taking all the rations and handing them out to the men. Once they figured out how we got them they went down and sealed all the hatches.

Once in a while you would hear a shrill whistling then someone talking through a microphone and say, "The smoking lamp is out." I said to my buddy if the smoking lamp is out why don't they light it? What they really meant was no smoking, because submarines are out and they might see a flicker of light and think there's something out there. I would occasionally hear the words starboard side or port side. I said, "What are they talking about?" I'd never heard those words before. I finally learned starboard is the right side of ship, port is left side.

We were on that ship, zig-zagging across the ocean, for thirty days, when we finally landed in Oran, Africa. We were there for about a week. The men and I had lost so much weight and most were seasick the whole way there. In Oran they told us to sleep with our rifles because the Arabs were sneaking in and stealing anything they could. There would be gunfire every night. It was from our own soldiers killing Arabs before they could get to us.

We got a pass to visit Casablanca and we visited a canteen, had food and drinks, and listened to music and dance. We had to be back at a certain time for pick up and if we weren't there, they left and were not coming back for us.

From there they shipped us off by train. They put us in cattle cars, eighty of us or so to one car. We couldn't even lie down to sleep; you had to sit with your knees up to try and sleep. When we passed through tunnels, we all started to choke from the smoke coming from the coal-fed engines. It was the longest three days of my life.

Finally we arrived in Algiers, where we stayed for one week. Many of the men got dysentery. Hundreds of men were running for the latrine. Some would suddenly stop in their tracks, and you had to laugh because you knew they didn't make it. One day they had called us all out for information. We were told that someone had stolen a truck load of mattress covers to sell to the Arabs on the black market for twenty dollars a cover. The Arabs would cut three holes in them, one for the head and two for the arms, and wear them as their garments. The people who stole the trucks were never caught. We were nearly starved in Algiers, too. We only got one meal a day. There was a place where we could buy big, beautiful oranges, and if you got there early enough in the morning, you'd get more than enough. If you weren't early you'd get nothing.

Two weeks later they took us back down to the port and put us on an English transport ship. It was a rusted old ship and was leaning pretty far over. I thought it was the *Merrimack* left over from the Civil War. We left that night, and when land was sighted, it was Italy. We landed in the Port of Naples. That left me with such a funny feeling because my mother and father were born in a town just outside of Naples called Altavilla. I told my friends that my parents had left from that port to come to America.

Chapter 4

Front Lines

It was now late December of 1943. After we landed in the port of Naples, they gave us our divisional badges and told us to sew them on. We were told we would be in the 36th Infantry Division, which is in the Fifth Army under General Mark Clark, otherwise known as the T-patchers. Later that night we were shipped out again. We couldn't travel during the day — it was too dangerous because we were so close to the front lines, near the abbey at Monte Cassino and the Rapido River. At the time, I knew nothing of what was in store for me at the River of Hell. A name I gave it after my experience there.

We were taken to Mussolini's race track to make camp. We finally were given something to eat — a stew of some sort. I didn't care, I was so hungry I could have eaten a horse — and I found out later I did. The meat looked different, it was red and stringy but not bad, sweet tasting. I later asked the cook what kind of meat it was, he answered, "You're at a horse track aren't you?" I couldn't believe the Army would feed us horse meat, after that I took off back to camp. I was moving at a pretty good trot. They could have been joking … I was never sure.

We were the replacements for the 36th (Texas) Infantry Division. I was placed in A Company of the 143rd Regiment. After a week we were loaded on trucks to join our new outfit, which was at the front lines at the bottom of a mountain. When we got there you could hear shooting going on, big stuff, not small stuff. We stayed there overnight, by this time it was January 1944 and it was cold. We dug our fox hole, lay in there, and slept if you could. Next morning we line up, just waiting. Three of us started to climb a mountain that was near. Finally they blew a whistle, yelling come on back down and get together, we're ready. A lieutenant not from our outfit said, "The three guys that climbed that mountain there, part-way, who were you, raise your hands." I'm thinking why to myself, why does he want to know why we climbed that mountain. Two of the guys raised their hands. I remembered my Sergeant from boot camp, Sergeant Feathercheck was his name. For some reason he liked me and taught me a lot. He said, "Son, never volunteer for anything." I'm glad I remembered so I didn't raise my hand. I just put my head down. He said, "There's one more guy, who is it?" Again I said nothing. I turned my head away from the other two guys hoping they wouldn't rat me out. They didn't. The lieutenant told the two guys to go with him. After they left I asked around as to why he took those two guys away. One of the guys said, "They're going to make mule skinners out of them." I said, "What are you talking about, mule skinners?" There are a lot of mountains to climb and they need men to guide the mules with ammunition and food to the top. I was happy to get out of that detail.

The trucks took us as far as they could, and then we had to walk on foot to the top of Mount Trocchio, about a quarter mile from Monte Cassino. Once we reached the top, we were told to setup our pup tents. That night I heard mail call, and we all gathered around the mailman to see if any letters had arrived from back home. They always made sure that we always got our mail, no matter where we were. It was good for morale. I had heard the captain tell the mailman when he came back from the mountain to our base camp, "Tell the cook to send up hot coffee and donuts for the men." Word came back that it was too late and too dangerous. The captain sent word back down to tell that cook to either send the coffee and donuts or to come himself. Later that day we were all enjoying hot coffee and donuts.

The next day the captain asked me to go down the mountain to the camp below and bring up a burner so we could make hot chocolate. The Army had given us chocolate bars so they could be melted down and made into hot chocolate. At the time there was gunfire over our heads and all I could think of was that I was going to die trying to bring a burner up for hot chocolate. I looked at the captain and said, "Captain, if you want hot chocolate you can go down the mountain and get the burner yourself." I thought, *Oh my God, what did I just do?* I thought for sure I would be in big trouble. After telling the guys what I said, I was told that no officer should ask you to do something he would not do himself. So nothing ever came of it.

THE ITALIAN CAMPAIGN

Chapter 5

The Battle

Our objective was to capture Monte Cassino. The Germans were dug in so deep there, it was like a fort. We didn't want to bomb the abbey, because there were monks there and it was a historic religious building. General Mark Clark was opposed to bombing. Nonetheless, three weeks after my fight there, on the morning of February 15, 1944 my regiment was at a rest area when all of a sudden we heard and saw flying over our heads 142 Boeing B-17 Flying Fortress heavy bombers, followed by 47 North American B-25 Mitchell and 40 Martin B-26 Marauder medium bombers. They had dropped 1,150 tons of high explosives and incendiary bombs on the abbey, reducing the entire top of Monte Cassino to a pile of rubble. Between bomb runs, the II Corps artillery pounded the mountain. Unfortunately this all took place after many lives were lost trying to capture Monte Cassino. I'm not sure if it would have made a difference but thinking back, I may not have lost my best friend or have been wounded if this bombing had happened earlier. Or, who knows, it could have been worse and I might have lost my life. In my eyes, the bombing was a mistake because that just left more hiding places for the Germans. When the war was over the abbey was rebuilt.

It was the 14th of January and it snowed about four inches that night, it was one of the worst winters Italy had in a long time. I was turning nineteen. I didn't tell anyone, didn't want them throwing me a party, as if they could have anyways. Anyhow we would go on watches, four hours on, four hours off. We were in a wooded area and to the right a plateau, it had big rocks. As you looked out you saw the Rapido River that lead across to Monte Cassino.

Now and then the Germans would lob a shell near us. There was a direct hit on one guy in our foxhole. He was only twenty or twenty-five feet from me. It got him right in the heart. He looked up at us and said, "Please, can you help me?" and died right there. That night for some reason I couldn't stop thinking of that kid.

In a matter of days orders came down from General Mark Clark once again that we would be making an attack on Monte Cassino and surround Sant'Angelo from the north and south. We were to make the main push across the Gustav Line, the German line of defense, by crossing the Rapido River, or the Bloody River as it was being called, and head towards the abbey. The plan was for two line regiments of the 36th, the 141st and the 143rd to cross the river for the attack. It was at 8:00 pm when we attempted to cross the river. We were told, "We're going to put out smoke pots so the Germans won't be able to see us. When they go off, stay close, and bunched in like bananas, because you won't be able to see a thing." You couldn't see your hand in front of your face, not only because of the smoke pots but because it was really foggy. We were holding onto each other's back packs to make sure we didn't wander off.

We hit the smoke and started through when, all of a sudden all hell broke loose. Mortars, machine gun fire, small arms fire lit up the sky. What I saw next would and still does haunt me. Oh my God, I saw piles of bodies, three and four piled up. Within a second, another would hit and I'd see the same thing — another pile of mangled bodies, missing hands and arms, even legs. Body parts everywhere. I said, "I don't want to see anymore," so I hit the ground and covered my head. The noise was horrific. I couldn't hear anything, no one was giving commands, so I said, "I've got to get out of here." So I proceeded forward and got to the river. It wasn't a wide river, about twenty-five to fifty feet wide and about twelve to fifteen feet deep. But on this day it was high, and the current was swift because of all the snow up in the mountains. I could see guys falling into the river and being swept downstream with all their equipment on from the foot bridges that our own engineers had built. I thought God how could they come up to swim anywhere and all I could hear were the screams of dying men. There was a bridge there, and we were among the first to make it to the river. I hit that bridge and, by God, it didn't take me any time at all to cross and get to the other side. When I hit the bank of the river I put my head down. I didn't want to put my head back up for fear it would get shot off. But I had to look! I needed to see if they would counterattack. I was there by myself; the rest were back there all charred up. Finally I heard the orders,

"Fall back!" I hit the bridge, I ran so fast and got across the river again and headed back up the mountain.

Since we were the lead battalion and were headed back to our start point, that allowed the Germans to concentrate all their fire to the northern crossing and the 1st Battalion of the 141st was stuck and never rescued and never to be heard from again.

I was cold, I was wet, and I was tired. I just put my head on my knees. I couldn't get out of my mind all I had seen that day. All I thought about all day was who came up with the idea of the smoke pots? All it did was alert the Germans to where we were. As I sat there with my head on my knees, the lieutenant came by and said, "Put some dry socks on and get some rest. We're going back tonight." I couldn't rest and I couldn't eat anything. It was January 22nd and at 4:00 pm we began our second attempt to cross the river. They said, "This time we're not going to put the smoke pots out." I thought, thank God.

For a second time we attempted again to cross the river. We got to the spot where all hell had broken loose and I had wanted to brace myself for it, but how do you brace yourself for something like that again? We finally got there … nothing. Not a shot was fired. We made it to the riverbank again, but this time somebody came up with another bright idea. Instead of the footbridges they had rubber pontoon rafts anchored to each side. So again our company was the lead for another attack, and our battalion was the first to cross the river by 6:35 pm.

Our commanding officer was a redhead. He replaced the Captain. We called him Lieutenant Spike. He called us together and told us, "I'm your new company commander. Most of you guys will be killed before I even learn your names." That didn't go over well with the guys. I don't think he should have said that, but he did and he was right.

Lieutenant Spike made his rounds earlier that day, he wanted to get acquainted with everybody and he came up to me and my buddy who I went through all of basic training with and said. "You two guys look so much alike I can't tell you apart, almost twins." He walked away then to meet the other guys in our unit.

Later we crossed the river on the rubber rafts, got to the riverbank and looked across. You could see the shadow of the abbey. There were only a few of us that had made it across. While sitting on the river bank waiting on the others the 2nd, lieutenant looked at me and said, "I'm putting together a special force unit and I want you there with me." Just as he was about to tell me what it was all about, he got the call to move forward. He said, "All right, let's go." So I got up and started to go with him. I was about fifty or sixty feet ahead and I looked to my left and there was my look-alike, about five feet to my left and a couple of feet behind me. I didn't see anybody else. Everybody was back at the river, still crossing. So far there were no shots from the Germans. They must have taken off, I thought to myself.

Seconds after, a shell hit behind me. The force of it blew me two feet into a drainage ditch full of water. I was stunned and for a minute I didn't know where I was, but I felt a pain behind me. I stuck my hand back there and my finger felt a hole, I was bleeding. My backpack was shattered, my shirt was torn up. I put my hand back there again and I felt another hole. I was hit in two places. I looked over at my look-alike. His whole back was shot out. He probably took the brunt of it, I knew he was gone. I'm not sure why, but for the life of me I just can't remember his name. It's been seventy years since this all has happened and for seventy years I have tried to remember his name. I think because of what I saw and the fact that he became my best buddy, I just blocked it from mind, and for that reason I cannot remember his name.

The lieutenant hollered over to me and said, "Are you guys all right?" I said, "No lieutenant, I'm hit in two places, and my buddy I think is gone." He said, "You get back to the river and get some help." I was so far away from everybody. How in the world am I going to make it back there? All the small arms fire, machine guns, everything was coming in heavy. All I could think of was my mother and how she would handle the news about me being wounded or even worse, especially just hearing about my older brother being wounded at the Battle of the Bulge. So I had to make a decision; either try to get some help or stay there and bleed to death. If I was alive in the morning, the Germans are going to get me. So I took a chance and started back. I was limping back and all I could hear was gunfire whizzing past me — through my legs, all around me. The good Lord must have been with me that day because how in the world I didn't get hit I'll never know.

I headed toward the pontoon boat so I could get back across and get some help when a shell hit to my left. I saw one of the GIs bounce about a foot off the ground. Instead of going to the boat and trying to get across the river, I detoured to him, because there was no one else around. I went over and leaned down and who do you think it was? It was Lieutenant Spike, yes the same man who said, "Most of you guys will be killed before I learn your name." There he was, lying there. He was shot up pretty bad and moaning. He must have taken a direct hit, but he wasn't dead.

I had spotted another soldier there, getting ready to go back across the river, I said, "Come here, it's Lieutenant Spike, and he's hurt real bad. We have to get him out of here or he's going to die." We carried him down to the river and put him in a raft and shimmied across the freezing cold water of the river. The raft had handles on the side, so we left Lieutenant Spike in the raft and climbed out and started to walk along the riverbank dragging the raft with Lieutenant Spike in it. I was hurting, but when you're scared you can do anything. We walked for miles before we ran into another soldier and asked him how far to the field hospital. He said, "Keep going straight and when you come to the bend turn left." So we did just that. It seemed to take forever but eventually we made it.

The field hospital was away from the front lines. When we got there, there were guys lying all over the place. The hospital was packed inside and out. I caught an orderly walking by and said, "I got the lieutenant here. He's shot up real bad." The orderly looked at him and said, "We're loaded inside, but we'll take him. How about you?" I said, "I'm hit in two places." "Will you be alright for a few minutes?" he asked. "Sure," I replied. It wasn't long before the orderly came back for me and put me on a stretcher. The doctors and nurses at the field hospital were fantastic. Nurses would talk to us and try to keep us calm. I will never forget what they did for me. They took me to the operating table and next thing I knew, I woke up in a hospital in Naples, Italy. I never knew if Lieutenant Spike made it or not.

I received the Bronze Star for my actions that day. But it took sixty years to get it. I did get my Purple Heart right away. I could have kept going back across the river alone, but I didn't — I knew I had to help the lieutenant. As for the lieutenant who wanted me for the special force unit, I never saw him again. I'm not sure what happened to him, so I never learned what the special force unit was about.

While recuperating in the hospital I thought of that kid who died in my arms and my best friend, and with nothing else to do I wrote a poem.

(poem as he wrote it)

A Friend Died

I crowled out of my hole, when the firing was done I looked for my friend but found only his gun. I looked all around but no one in sight, only the dead men who died in the fight.

I herd someone call in the still of the night, there lie my friend neath the stars so bright, I knelt by his side and I picked up his head he looked in my face and the last words he said, please write to my mother and let her know that God has called and I must suddenly go. He gave a last breath and he gave a last sigh and the tears ran down from my eyes. Oh please God in heaven take care of my friend, it wasn't his fault that his life had to end. And now that he's gone I feel that I'm lost all get them old jerries no matter the cost.

Sixty years later a friend of mine gave me a book about my division. It had everyone's names in it, where they were from, and if they were killed in action (KIA), missing in action (MIA), lightly injured in action (LIA), died of wounds (DOW), seriously wounded in action (SWA), lightly wounded in action (LWA), and seriously injured in action (SIA). I saw Lieutenant Spike's name: Francis Gorman from Massachusetts, WIA. January 22, 1944. He made it, I said to myself. Even after getting the book and looking through all the names, I still couldn't remember my friend's name. It's still a block for me.

The 36th Division had failed in their attempt to cross the Rapido River. Their assault was intended to break through to the Lira Valley, with the 1st Armored Division to follow behind on January 20, 1944. After trying to maintain a foothold on the north side of the river, the assault was called off on the 22nd and by 1800 hours all officers were casualties except for one. It was confirmed that 500 were captured by the 15th Panzergrenadier Division.

The 36th Infantry Division suffered dearly on their two-day assault. Of the 6,000 men who participated, 2,128 were casualties, including 550 dead.

THE ITALIAN CAMPAIGN

CROSSING THE GARIGLIANO
AND RAPIDO RIVERS
17 January-8 February 1944

ALLIED ADVANCE
GERMAN UNIT

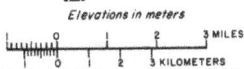

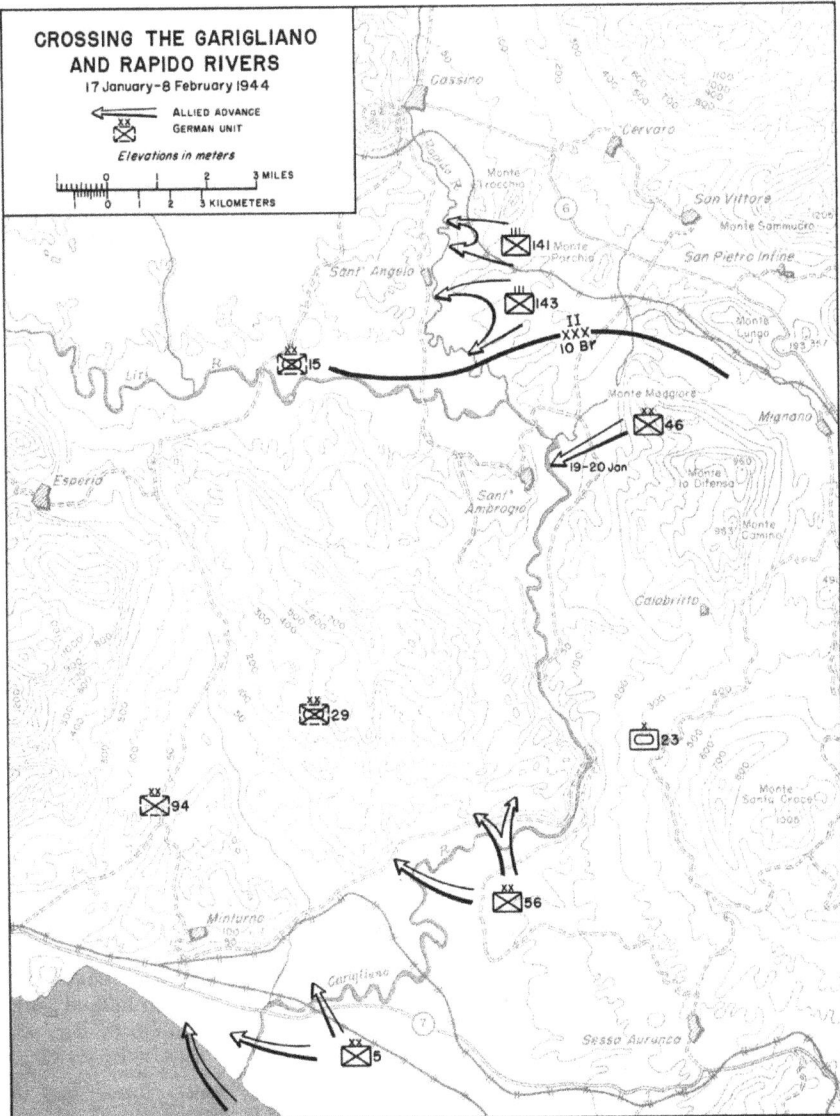

Elevations in meters

0   1   2   3 MILES
0   1   2   3 KILOMETERS

Chapter 6

Back to My Division

After my stay in the hospital they sent me back to my outfit that was in a rest area, and everybody was new. Out of my platoon, there were only six of us who came back alive. The rest of them were either killed or wounded so bad that they weren't able to return.

One day while at the rest area I decided to take a walk by myself. As I was walking, I noticed two civilians following me. The longer they followed, the more nervous I became. I just knew they wanted to rob me. I turned around and started to speak Italian and asked them if they knew where the town of Altavilla was. I then explained that my mother and father were born there. They said "No" — they didn't know where the town was and then took off running in the field. About that time a truckload of British soldiers were driving by and I was able to flag them down. They picked me up and took me back to my camp.

A few days later a sergeant came to me and handed me a Springfield .03 World War I rifle and said, "Come with me." He took me to a firing range and told me to shoot at the targets one thousand feet away. I sensed right away that they wanted to make a sniper out of me, so I purposely missed every target. I wasn't going to let them put me in a tree like a monkey to be shot at.

Three of us were sent out one day to patrol the area for the enemy. We were told to be careful of landmines. As we were walking we noticed a farmhouse, and as we got close a gentleman came out and started hanging up white sheets on a laundry line. When he finished he went back into the farmhouse. Not thinking anything of it at the time, we continued on. A few minutes later we were bombarded with artillery. We ran towards the river, jumped over the side, and hugged the bank of the river. We waited there till the firing was over. We wanted to return to that farmhouse to set it on fire because we knew then that the gentleman was alerting the enemy, but we didn't have time. We ran back to the camp to notify them that we located the enemy. We told the officers what had happened and they notified other platoons in the area.

Later we left our camp and headed toward the mountain. Every hour we were able to take a fifteen minute break. At one point, at one of our rest stops, they called us all together and told us we were going to go on a night hike and were to go full- backpack, which weighed about forty pounds. It was cold and raining, so they told us to put on our rain gear and form together. We got to the bottom of the mountain and were told when we got to the top we were to pitch our tents and stay all night.

But my buddies and I never made it to the top because of a shining light coming from the woods. I said to them, "Let's go check out that light." At first they didn't want to go, but they ended up following me. As we got closer, we realized the light was coming from inside a small house. We went to the house and I knocked on the door. An elderly man came to the door. I was able to communicate with the man and let him know we weren't there to do him any harm. We were hungry and cold and asked if he had anything to eat. He let us in and gave us wine, and fresh baked homemade bread, and warm chestnuts. We scrounged up whatever little money we had and gave it to the man. He thanked us and then I asked, "Could we sleep here tonight?" The old man was hesitant, you could tell, but he shook his head yes.

My buddies really didn't want to stay for fear of getting in trouble. I told them I would much rather sleep on a warm floor out of the cold than sleep outside on wet ground. So we did. We woke up to the noise of trucks and the rest of our regiment coming up the mountain. We ran out of the back of the small house and just got in line with the rest of the regiment coming up the mountain. The captain turned around and said, "Where have you guys been? We've been looking for you." I said, "What are you talking about? We've been here the whole time."

He gave us a look and said, "Get in the truck." The three of us just sat there and laughed while everyone else was trying to figure out why we were laughing. We got away with it and we knew it. Every time we would see each other after that we would start to laugh.

When we came off the front lines we never set up camp near a city or town. As meals were being cooked for lunchtime, we could see children standing there outside the camp. They would wait for any leftovers they could have. The cook always made sure to give them what he could. Their small thin bodies and the look on their faces always made me cry. I grew up during the Depression and we had it bad but never that bad. We were poor but didn't know it.

Chapter 7

The Ruins of Old Pompeii

One day my battery decided to go and visit the ruins of Old Pompeii. There were cities and buildings and even people buried under the ash of Mount Vesuvius, a volcano that erupted in 79A.D. Behind a glass enclosure you could see a woman holding her infant child in her arms, covered in ash. It was the way they died, and it had been preserved for thousands of years. As we walked through more buildings, we admired what they were able to do with a block of marble and stone, and all it took was a hammer and chisel.

We left there to visit the new Pompeii when the volcano started acting up. We put on parkas and hoods and four-buckle boots as we walked through a half an inch of soot. While we continued looking for other buildings, the volcano got worse — it suddenly got dark as the volcano blocked out the sun. I turned to the guys and said, "We better get out of here before this volcano blows its top or they will be digging us up and putting us behind enclosed glass." I can see it now: 'Here lie stupid American soldiers caught in the eruption of the volcano.'

Chapter 8

Famiglia

I was able to get a pass one day to go into a town called Avellino. I had heard my mother and father talk about that town many times as a kid. I went into the canteen there where they had anisette, cognac, or wine. No beer or anything else but that didn't matter, I wasn't a drinker. While in there an American GI comes around and he says, "Hey, is anybody here from around Pittsburgh?" I said, "Yeah, I'm from the outskirts, why, who wants to know?" He says "There's a little Italian guy over here that's been asking everybody if there's anybody here from Pittsburgh." I went over to the man and started talking to him, he was amazed at how well I spoke the language. As sure as God made green apples this man was my mother's first cousin. He said "Oh my God, you have to come to my house." I don't remember his name but I know he was my mother's cousin. He says, "You have to come by the house, I'm going to call the town, Altavilla Irpina, and tell them you're here." Because there was no transportation he went home and brought back a horse and wagon. We went to his house to call the family. It was hard making a connection so it took a while. He finally got through to the town where my mother and father were born and told them I was there. He said, "They want to see you." I said, "I can't right now I've got to get back to camp, I will see if I can come back soon."

So I went back to camp only to find out that we had to move and set up camp somewhere else. When I got there I saw this captain that I knew and occasionally who I would share my cigars from home with. They were Marsh & Wheeling cigars that my mother and father would send me. I would give him one or two because I knew he liked smoking them like I did. Knowing one day I might need a favor I didn't mind sharing my cigars with him. So I went to him and said, "Listen, I got relatives not too far from here, uncles, aunts, cousins. I would like a pass to go." He said, "Well, I'll tell you what. I don't know, we got orders to ship out, but I'll give you a pass for two days." That's all I can do, and if you're not back we will leave without you, none of us know where we're going yet."

So I go to the train station and as luck would have it they were running. They had big picture windows and were all electric, no steam engines. They had green velvet seats and were very comfortable. You could hardly hear the train pulling out it was so quiet. I went as far as Foggia and got off the train there. I remembered my dad's story as a kid he would take the family mule and go there to sell figs. Anyways I told a guy there," I'm going to Altavilla Irpina," and he said, "Well, it's a distance from here, on the mountain over there." I said, "Well, can I get a bus?" He says, "Bus? You want to get there, you walk." Because all the bridges were out and there was no other transportation. I said, "Well, I'm here now." He said, "Take this road." So I started to walk and it was a long walk at that. I was glad I only had my backpack and not my gun that, would have made it seem much longer.

I happened to run into a fellow on the road along the way and stopped to talk to him. I asked, "Do you know where the town of Altavilla Irpina is?" He said, "Yes, it sits on that mountain up there." So I asked, "Do you know the DeFazio family?" He said, "Well, I don't know people from up there, but do you see that farmhouse down there? Why don't you go down and ask him, he probably knows." So I go to the farmhouse and knock on the door. A man comes to the door and I tell him I'm heading up the mountain to Altavilla and that I have relatives there. I said, "Mi chiamo Alberto DeFazio." I said my mother's name is Giuseppina Galasso. He says, "Galasso? Oh my God, you're my sister's son!" He grabbed me, brought me inside, and says, "You stay and eat something first, before I take you to meet everybody." After we ate he took me to meet my mother's sister. Then he took me to meet my father's brother. I stayed the night there. I kept thinking this was all a dream. I mean, who comes all this way to fight a war and runs into family they have never met. The next day I went to meet my aunt, my father's sister, and she was a beautiful woman and very nice. While there I ate homemade fusillis, which here you know as macaronis. I also got to meet my godfather who baptized me while in America in the 1920s. He had to go back to Italy because he had a wife and kids. He had worked for the water company for a while before returning. My godfather had given me a gold pocket watch when he baptized me, still have it, I gave it to my son. My godfather and I walked all around and he spoke English to me the whole time.

Even though I was an American in an American uniform they looked past that. I was family here, I met cousin after cousin. I have no clue how many I met. I still have cousins there and in Rome, even South America and Canada.

Chapter 9

Invasion of Anzio

When I got back to camp they said that we were shipping out and going to Anzio. The 3rd Division went in first at Anzio, and there was no resistance. Maybe a shot or two was fired, that's it. Then we stopped and dug in, which was the worst thing we could have done. Ahead of us was a mountain, and on the other side was Rome. If we had kept going we would have had the high ground at the mountain, but we stopped for a couple nights. In the meantime, the Germans were moving their panzer division from Monte Cassino to try and stop us. If we had made it to Rome it would have been all over for them.

While we were stopped, we heard a loud noise. We looked up in the sky and there was a shell that came by that was as big as a small car. That shell whizzed right by and when it hit it left a hole big enough to build a foundation of a house.

They sent out patrols to try and contact the Germans. I went out with a couple of guys. We didn't run into anybody, so we bivouacked that night – dug our foxhole. When we were on the march again, the sergeant said to me, "DeFazio, you're going to take the point." As the point, I was the one guy out there by himself. The guy behind me was about fifty yards back, and behind him was the rest of our unit. I don't know why they didn't, but they should have just called you the sacrificial lamb because that's what you were. If you were shot, then the rest of the platoon knew it wasn't safe to go any further. I said to myself, "Well, thank you very much, I'll remember you in my will." Praying that wouldn't be for a long time.

As I was walking, all I could think of was, "If I come by any German I could only hope and pray he was cross-eyed and can't shoot straight. Along the side of the road I saw a young German soldier lying there dead, and I felt so sorry for him. The Germans were moving so fast that they just left him there. They didn't even have to time to pick this poor soul up. Even though he was the enemy, I felt bad, thinking he might have a family back home. He didn't want to be here, the same as everybody else.

So there I was, out there alone and scared. Well, thank God we didn't run into anybody. Later we ran into the main German force, and that's when we dug our foxholes again. There was scattered small arms fire coming in when all of a sudden one of our tanks came up alongside my foxhole. We started hollering, "Get that tank out of here!" It was drawing all the fire toward us. It was hit so many times the noise was tremendous.

We fell back, and all of a sudden everything hit. Artillery was coming in and shaking the ground. The trees were flying, and my head was just ringing. I was lying on the ground and they were firing all around me. I must have been shell-shocked. A medic was nearby and took me back to a farmhouse where there were wounded guys everywhere. One guy's belly was split, and his bladder was sticking out. With tears in my eyes I watched them try to push it back in and it wouldn't go. Finally, they gave me a pill that knocked me out, and the next thing I knew I was back at the field hospital. When I woke up, the doctor told me I had a concussion. He said, "Son, we're not sending you back to your outfit, but we are sending you back to the States." It was only a matter of days when our Army had marched into Rome and the battle in Italy was over.

Chapter 10

Back to the States

The Italian theater was a grueling a campaign as anything in World War II and worse than most. The Battle of the Bloody River was its saddest of moments for the Americans.

When I got back to the States I was lucky enough to be sent to South Park, Pennsylvania, not far from Pittsburgh and not far from my hometown of Verona. I saw the Army doctor when I arrived and told him I was having bad headaches and nightmares. He said nothing, and nothing was ever done about it. The headaches went away but the nightmares continued.

Every day we went through close order drills given by the sergeant. Now and then he would pick one of the men to do the drill; most often he picked me because I was good at it. Once in a while they would place one of us with a city police officer who would be directing traffic. We always looked forward to lunch time because we were treated to lunch by the officer. Often they would send us out in the Army trucks to patrol the city.

I was able to get a pass one day to go home. While I was there a few friends had talked me into going to Verona's local bar, Terri's Place. I'm not a drinker and never was, but once in a while I'll have a beer or a glass of homemade Italian wine that's made by my brother. My friends and people I didn't even know kept buying me drinks all night, and I got so drunk I could barely stand or walk. Finally, my friends took me to the bus stop and put me on a bus and told the driver to make sure I made it to downtown. I was so sick that I could hardly hold my head up. I remember a young couple on the bus held my head up for me the whole ride into town. I'm not sure how I did it, but I happened to get on the right streetcar to take me to Castle Shannon. Once I got there I was to wait on an Army truck to take me back to the base. When I got there, there were other soldiers waiting too. I was shivering from the cold night air. There was a woman there who said to me, "Soldier, are you cold?"

"Yes ma'am, I'm freezing," I replied. She was a large, heavyset woman and was wearing a long fur coat. She came over to me, opened the coat and put her arms around me to keep me warm. It wasn't much longer afterwards the Army truck came to pick us up.

Once in the truck, all the other soldiers were laughing and making fun of me. "You should have seen yourself!" they said. "This little head was all you could see sticking out from this woman's coat." All I could think of was go ahead and laugh, at least I was warm.

One day I decided on my own to go home and see my family, only this time I went without permission. The next day the Captain called me into his office and said, "DeFazio, I was going to promote you to drill sergeant, but since you left without a pass I can't do that now." He put me on detention for a week.

Soon we shipped out to Fort Story, Virginia. From there they sent us to a depot where they brought in boxcars filled with vegetables and frozen foods. Trucks came everyday to pick up the food and deliver it to different Army bases. Our food went to Fort Story and what they didn't want came back to us for our portions. I didn't appreciate that, so one day I took it upon myself and went into the freezer. I saw that there were wooden barrels filled with turkeys. I smashed the top of one of the barrels and took out the biggest turkey I could find and brought it to the cook. "Where did you get this turkey?" The cook asked. "From the freezer." "You're going to get in a lot of trouble." Yet again nothing ever came of it. From then on we ate what we wanted and, believe me, we ate the best. I loved it there and why not? There were no officers, no drills to do, and we did pretty much what we wanted. From there I was then discharged.

Chapter 11

Home Again

When I got home I was going to reenlist to go over to the Pacific, but the Army said I was eligible to get out on the point system. I did just that.

Two weeks after returning home I had gone to work again for the water company. I remember saying to my father one day, "Pop, don't you want to go back to Italy and visit your family?" He said, "There's nothing back there for me, son." His mother was still alive, but he felt that America had so much more to offer.

As far as I'm concerned, I would rather sleep in a gutter in this country than live in any other country in the world. I'm not looking for glory or recognition. I had a job to do and I did it. The U.S. at times may consider itself the moral voice of the world, but many other countries in the world have benefited from following America's lead. The young men that died over there didn't die in vain. They died to make us free, to provide a good life for us, and to let us sleep well at night.

I had seen a lot of sadness, endured a lot of pain during my time in Italy, but it wasn't all bad — it was a good experience. You couldn't buy that education for $100,000, so I don't regret it. I just felt sorry for the ones that didn't make it back.

It took years before I could sleep through the night. The nightmares were awful. I stayed single for ten years. In 1954 I ended up meeting my wife, Freda, on a blind date. I knew she was the one and we were married six months later. In 1956 my daughter Valerie was born and three years later my son Albert was born. We have four grandchildren and two great grandchildren. After a long illness suffering from Rheumatoid arthritis and fifty-two years of marriage, my wife passed away on July 3, 2007. Once in a while I'll still have a nightmare but not often. For years I would startle easily and not know why. It took sixty years before I found out it was post traumatic stress syndrome. I lived my life with no regrets. I served my country and they owe me nothing. God Bless America.

Chapter 12

Honorable Mention

Charles E. Kelly

My daughter had asked if there was anyone else from our area that fought in the Italian Campaign that I may have known. There were several, but I never knew them well. But one name came to mind: Charles "Commando" Kelly, the one-man army. I never had the chance to meet Charles Kelly, but I thought it might be fitting to mention him in my story because of our mutual connection to Pittsburgh and military service in Italy.

Kelly was born and raised in Pittsburgh, not far from me. He joined the Army in May 1942; he was a part of my regiment. In September of 1943 he was serving as a Corporal in Company L, 143rd Infantry Regiment, 36th Infantry Division. Kelly had voluntarily participated in several patrols on September 13th near Altavilla, Italy. He helped defend an ammunition storehouse against attack by the German forces. He had held his position all night inside the building. When withdrawal became necessary, Kelly voluntarily stayed behind and held the German soldiers at bay until everyone had been evacuated from the storehouse. He then rejoined the unit.

Charles E. Kelly was awarded the Congressional Medal of Honor on February 18, 1944, for his actions that day. He died on January 11, 1985, at age sixty-four.

Chapter 13

General Mark Clark

Mark Wayne Clark was born May 1, 1896. General Clark was an American general during World War II and the Korean War and was the youngest three-star general in the U.S. Army.

I never met him personally, but I was able to catch a glimpse of him one day when his small Piper Cub plane landed at camp. He was a tall, thin man, very distinguished looking. After the huge loss of men at the Rapido River, the 36th "Texas" Infantry Division didn't think very much of the General. They were very angry and couldn't forget what happened as they fought their way through Europe.

On March 2, 1944 twenty-five members of the 36th Division met in an Italian cattle barn. They were celebrating Texas Independence Day. These men drew up a resolution which dealt with their experiences at the River of Hell just a few weeks before. The resolution called for an investigation of the Rapido River crossing and General Mark Clark's order that caused so many useless and unnecessary casualties. These twenty-five men decided to postpone any action because they feared that controversy over this would endanger the war effort.

The 36th Division Association held its first meeting in Brownwood, Texas, on January 19, 1946 which was on the second anniversary of the crossing of the Rapido River, a military undertaking that will go down in history as one of the colossal blunders of World War II.

by Clayton D. Laurie

At 10 a.m. on March 18, 1946, Andrew J. May, chairman of the Military Affairs Committee of the House of Representatives, called to order hearings on the Rapido River crossing conducted by the 36th Infantry Division near Sant' Angelo, Italy, between January 20 and 22, 1944.

During the course of two days of hearings, the 30 committee members heard testimony from veterans supporting the statements made in two resolutions: one approved in January 1946 by the members of the 36th Infantry Division Association and the other passed by the Texas Legislature. These resolutions referred to the infamous battle as "one of the most colossal blunders of the Second World War," a "murderous blunder" that "every man connected with this undertaking knew … was doomed to failure" before it took place.

Further, the resolutions charged Lt. Gen. Mark W. Clark, the commander of the Fifth Army, of which the 36th Division was then a part, with a clear disregard for human life and military information. Clark, they alleged, ordered the attack even though he knew it was going to fail with horrendous losses, even after his subordinates had voiced their misgivings and offered alternative suggestions for attacks elsewhere that could, and later did, succeed. The petitioners urged Congress to investigate not just the "Rapido River fiasco," but to take "the necessary steps to correct a military system that will permit an inefficient and inexperienced officer, such as Gen. Mark Clark, in a high command … to prevent future soldiers from being sacrificed wastefully and uselessly." With this testimony and supplemental reports from the War Department and Secretary of War Robert P. Patterson, the committee examined all aspects of the Rapido River disaster …

Clark was completely exonerated, as it would have been inconceivable to find a four-star general guilty of incompetence.

The 36th finished their business of war as they fought through Italy, France, Germany and Austria. Even though they lost the battle with Clark for allowing such a fiasco, it still tarnished his career. The "Texas Army" served with courage and loyalty and no enemy could defeat that and I was a part of it.

The Men of A Company

Baird, Burnes T.................2nd Lt. ....SWA 22 Jan. 44... Clairton, PA
Gorman, Francis J. ....1st Lt. ....SWA 22 Jan. 44 .. Lynn, MA
Pliska, Richard J. ....2nd Lt. ..LWA 22 Jan. 44 . Two Rivers, WI
Upchurch, Richard J. ......2nd Lt. ..SWA 22 Jan. 44 .. Chicago, IL
Walker, David M. ....2nd Lt. ..LWA 22 Jan. 44 . Andover, NJ
Ables, James W. ....Pvt. ....LWA 21 Jan. 44 . Athens, TN
Ahl, Floyd A. ....Pvt. ....LWA 21 Jan. 44 . Schenectady, NY
Albanese, John J. ....Pvt. ....MIA 22 Jan. 44 ... Brooklyn, NY
Albano, Gaetano T. ....Pvt. ....SWA 27 Jan. 44 .. Brooklyn, NY
Alexander, Raymond .....Pvt. ....SWA 22 Jan. 44 .. Quincy, IL
Allonardo, Frank ....Pvt. ....LWA 21 Jan.44 .. Philadelphia, PA
Anderson, Anders G. ......Pvt. ....SWA 22 Jan. 44 .. Lynn, MA
Andriola, Vincent J. ....Pvt. ....LWA 23 Jan. 44 . Newark, NJ
Armstrong, Lewis H. ......Pfc. ....MIA 22 Jan. 44 ... Pilot Mountain, NC
Aylor, Robert L. ....Pvt. ....MIA 22 Jan. 44 ... Lawrenceburg, IN
Barnes, Homer E. ....Pfc. ....LWA 21 Jan. 44 . Ossing, NY
Bartko, Emil J. ....Pvt. ....LWA 22 Jan. 44 . Cleveland, OH
Bastain, Ralph A. ....Pvt. ....SWA 20 Jan. 44 .. Cleveland, OH
Baugher, Harold O. ....Pvt. ......LWA 22 Jan. 44 . Warsaw, IN
Beaver, Charles L. ....Pvt. ....SWA 22 Jan. 44 .. Lewner, GA
Beaver, Rufus A. ....Pvt. ....DOW 24 Jan. 44 . Lincolnton, NC
Bender, Wesley E. ....T/Sgt. ...MIA 22 Jan 44 .... Easton, PA
Betke, Albert H. ....Pvt. ....SWA 22 Jan. 44 .. Beaver Falls, PA
Blankenship, Clifton ....Pvt. ....LWA 27 Jan. 44 . Ashland, KY
Blanton, Gary F. ....Pfc. ....MIA 22 Jan. 44 ... Tabor City, NC
Blaschak, Frank A., Jr. ....Pvt. ....MIA 22 Jan. 44 ... Russellton, PA
Blewitt, David G. ....Pfc. ....SWA 22 Jan. 44 .. Dalton, PA
Bloch, Joseph ....Pvt. ....LWA 21 Jan. 44 . Chicago, IL
Boeglin, Eugene R. ....Pvt. ....LWA 22 Jan. 44 . N. Andover, MA
Bouchard, Lawrence A. ..Pfc. ....LWA 22 Jan. 44 .. Sherman Station, ME
Boucher, Samuel R. ....Pvt. ....MIA 22 Jan. 44 ... Bloomington, IN
Bowen, James C. ....Pvt. ....LWA 22 Jan. 44 . Lugoff, SC
Boyles, Grady J. ....Pvt. ....SWA 27 Jan. 44 .. Russelville, AL
Brann, Newton R. ....Pfc. ....LWA 22 Jan. 44 . Anderson, IN
Breeden, Lawrence ....Pvt. ....SWA 23 Jan. 44 .. Seiverville, TN
Brennan, George R. ....Pvt. ....SWA 22 Jan. 44 .. Clearspring, MD
Brewer, William S. ....Pfc. ....SWA 22 Jan. 44 .. Chicago, IL

Budd, Alfred G. .... Pvt. ....LWA 22 Jan. 44 .. Delaplane, VA
Buzard, Frederick A. ...... Pvt. ....LWA 22 Jan. 44 .. Cochranton, PA
Camello, Anthony J. .... Pvt. ....SWA 22 Jan. 44 .. Brooklyn, NY
Chapman, Campbell N. . Pfc. ....MIA 25 Jan. 44 ... Honea Path, SC
Coggins, James C., Jr. ..... Pvt. ....LWA 25 Jan. 44 .. Elizabethton, TN
Coleman, Lee A. .... Pfc. ....MIA 22 Jan. 44 ... Missouri Valley, IA
Collins, Clarence E. .... S/Sgt. ....LWA 22 Jan. 44 .. Pueblo, CO
Conn, Norman D. .... Pvt. ....MIA 22 Jan. 44 ... Kankakee, IL
Cook, Bill G. .... Pvt. ....SWA 27 Jan. 44 .. Kansas City, KS
Counts, Clyde D. .... Pvt. ....LWA 22 Jan. 44 .. Flintville, TN
Dansicker, Herbert .... Pfc. ....SWA 21 Jan. 44 .. Baltimore, MD
Davis, Jerry W. .... T/Sgt. ...LWA 22 Jan. 44 .. Paris, Texas
DeFazio, Albert .... Pfc. ....SWA 22 Jan. 44 .. Verona, PA
DeSanto, Joseph M. .... Pvt. ....KIA 22 Jan. 44 .... Plainfield, NJ
DeSimone, Salvatore P. . Pvt. ....LWA 21 Jan. 44 .. Bronx, NY
Dittman, Meredith E. ..... Pfc. ....SWA 21 Jan. 44 .. Buffalo, NY
Dixon, Arthur M. .... Pvt. ....MIA 22 Jan. 44 ... Dorchester, MA
Edwards, Albert E. .... Pvt. ....LWA 22 Jan. 44 .. Miami, OK
Fallon, Gerard M. .... Pvt. ....KIA 26 Jan 44 ..... Brooklyn, NY
Fields, Delbert M. .... Pvt. ....SWA 21 Jan. 44 .. Springfield, IN
Frederick, William O. .... S/Sgt. ....SWA 22 Jan. 44 .. Tyler, Texas
Galloway, Harold L. ...... S/Sgt. ....SWA 22 Jan. 44 .. Alto, Texas
Gannon, Edward C. .... Pvt. ....LWA 21 Jan. 44 .. Canton, OH
Graniere, Frank .... S/Sgt. ....LWA 22 Jan. 44 .. San Antonio, TX
Gray, Orval .... Pvt. ....LWA 22 Jan. 44 .. Henshaw, KY
Jellick, Charles T. .... S/Sgt. ....LWA 25 Jan. 44 .. Philadelphia, PA
Kaiser, Howard H. .... Sgt. ....MIA 22 Jan. 44 ... Brooklyn, NY
Kemp, John W. .... Pfc. ....SWA 22 Jan. 44 .. Ft. Wayne, IN
Kieczkajlo, Martin S. ...... Sgt. ....SWA 22 Jan. 44 .. New York, NY
Laiche, Anicet A. .... S/Sgt. ....MIA 22 Jan. 44 ... Paulina, LA
Lake, Scott .... Pfc. ....LWA 21 Jan. 44 .. Jamestown, IN
Lebeis, Bertram H. .... 1st. Sgt. .LWA 22 Jan. 44 .. New York, NY
Long, Jerry T. .... Pvt. ....MIA 22 Jan. 44 ... Corning, IA
McClintock, Archie S. .... Pvt. ....LWA 21 Jan. 44 .. Carlilse, PA
Markiewica, Walter J. .... S/Sgt. ....SWA 22 Jan. 44 .. Hamtramck, MI
Michalak, John J., Jr. .... Pvt. ....LWA 24 Jan. 44 .. Chicago, IL
Mitchell, James L. .... Pvt. ....LWA 21 Jan. 44 .. Hamilton, AL
Moffit, Harvey L. .... Pvt. ....SWA 22 Jan. 44 .. Ripley, MS
Monaco, Anthony R. ...... Sgt. ....LWA 21 Jan. 44 .. Chicago, IL
Nahodil, Robert S. .... Sgt. ....SWA 22 Jan. 44 .. Berea, OH
Naill, Kenneth B. .... Pvt. ....LWA 22 Jan. 44 .. Rockford, IL
Nuhfer, Harvey L. .... Pvt. ....SWA 27 Jan. 44 .. Toledo, OH
Parrot, William F. .... T/Sgt. ...LWA 24 Jan. 44 .. Garrison, Texas
Phillips, Frederick W. .... Pfc. ....LWA 21 Jan. 44 .. Long Branch, NJ

Pierco, Claude H. ....Pvt. ....MIA 22 Jan. 44 ... Coustok, MI
Roycroft, Alton R. ....Cpl. ....SWA 22 Jan. 44 .. Rusk, Texas
Sipes, James B. ....Pvt. ....MIA 22 Jan. 44 ... Hornsby, TN
Smith, Clarence W. ....Pvt. ....SWA 25 Jan. 44 .. Parkers Landing, PA
Sniezek, Edward A. ....Pfc. ....SWA 22 Jan. 44 .. Detroit, MI
Southard, Rodney N. ......Pvt. ....MIA 22 Jan. 44 ... Rochester, NH
Spencer, Kenneth R. ....Pvt. ....LWA 21 Jan. 44 . Bemis, TN
Stackhouse, Walter C. .....Pfc. ....LWA 22 Jan. 44 . Coatsville, PA
Stalnaker, Thomas ....Pvt. ....LWA 22 Jan. 44 . E. Tallassee, AL
Sternberg, William R. .....Pvt. ....MIA 22 Jan. 44 ... Newark, NJ
Stubblefield, James E. .....Pfc. ....LWA 21 Jan. 44 . Troup, Texas
Stults, Barney N. ....Pfc. ....LWA 25 Jan. 44 . Weatherford, TX
Sweatt, Paul L. ....Pvt. ....SWA 22 Jan. 44 .. Herald White, IL
Taylor, Joseph H. ....Sgt. ....SWA 22 Jan. 44 .. Brooklyn NY
Tellez, Joe R. ....Pvt. ....LWA 22 Jan. 44 . Los Angeles, CA
Terra, Antone E. ....Pvt. ....SWA 25 Jan 44 ... Taunton, MA
Thomas, Hilary S. ....Pvt. ....KIA 26 Jan. 44 ... Reed, KY
Treadway, Walker ....Pvt . ...LWA 22 Jan. 44 . Oak Hill, WV
Turner, John R. ....Pvt. ....LWA 22 Jan. 44 . Heflin, AL
Van Matre, Norman R. ...Pvt. ....SWA 22 Jan. 44 .. Kaylong, WV
Vaughn, Jack H. ....Pvt. ....LWA 20 Jan. 44 . Gadsden, AL
Vigil, Joe ....Pvt. ....LWA 24 Jan. 44 . Pueblo, CO
Vincent, Charles L. ....Pvt. ....SWA 21 Jan. 44 .. Louisville, KY
Walton, Alvin F. ....Pvt. ....MIA 22 Jan. 44 ... Buchannon, WV
Weissemeir, Raymond J. Pfc. ....LWA 25 Jan. 44 . Richmond Hill, NY
West, Warren J. ....Pfc. ....MIA 22 Jan. 44 ... Knoxville, TN

These are the men of my company only not included on the list are 605 names that were listed as missing in action. There were 18 officers and 587 enlisted men. Some of these men I trained with at Camp Shelby, the same men that almost left without me if I had not gone to my superiors and begged to go. I trusted them and they became my brothers through all my travels. It only took several days to watch them perish, one by one. After seventy years their names are gone from my memory but their faces are still embedded in my mind.

143rd U.S. Infantry Regiment ("Third Texas") 1917

MOTTO: "Arms secure peace" — "secure," as in "making something safe and secure."

FORMATION: The 143rd U. S. Infantry was officially formed at Camp Bowie, Texas, on October 15, 1917, from Texas troops drawn largely from the 3rd and 5th Texas National Guard Infantry Regiments. The Third Texas had been mobilized prior to the beginning of the war, serving along the Mexican border with troops from Harlingen to Roma and later near Corpus Christi. The troops of the 143rd arrived in France in the early summer of 1918, training near Bar-sur-Aube.

MEUSE-ARGONNE: As part of the 72nd Infantry Brigade, the 143rd entered the reserve of the French Armies of the Center on September 26, 1918, and later went into the line on October 3rd, relieving a regiment of the U.S. 2nd Division. They came under fire on

October 10, 1917, and fought through several days of bitter battle to gain the northern bank of the Aisne River by October 12. The regiment was relieved from front line duty on October 28, and all the regiments of the 36th Division were put in the reserve of the First American Army until the Armistice.

BETWEEN THE WARS, 1922-1940: The Regiment participated in disaster work when a great tidal wave struck Nueces, San Patricio and Aransas Counties. Units of the Regiment were called to activity duty due to the New London school disaster of 1937.

WORLD WAR II: Mobilized November 25, 1940. Trained at Camp Bowie, Brownwood, the second camp to be named for the hero of the Alamo. Although ready for overseas movement by July 1942, it trained with the Division at Camp Blanding, Florida, and Fort Edwards, Massachusetts. The 143rd was not shipped overseas until April 2, 1943, landing in Algeria.

Salerno/Liri Valley: In September, 1943, the Regiment went ashore near Salerno (Paestum), fighting one of the bloodiest battles of the unit's history. Later, in December 1943, the Regiment assaulted the "Winter Line" near San Pietro, with the First and Second Battalions receiving a Fifth Army Commendation for their valor. The capture of San Pietro by 36th Division troops opened the Liri Valley, breaking the "Winter Line." The Regiment endured a bloody failure in the crossing of the Rapido River in January 1944, suffering more casualties than it did in any like period during the entire war.

Anzio: The 143rd reinforced Fifth Army in the Anzio beachhead on the 19th of May 1944, and, as part of the breakout, moved rapidly around to the rear of Velletri on June 1, 1944, and arrived at the outskirts of Rome where they were told to "hold until other units could catch up."
Southern France: In August 1944, the Regiment was part of the 36th Division landing on Green Beach on the south coast of France. They marched 200 miles the first week, and soon — with the 141st — were part of the "Rhone River Bottleneck," virtually destroying the fleeing German Nineteenth Army. Fighting northeastward the 36th served as the right flank division of the Seventh Army.

Vosges and Germany, 1944-45: After the liberation of Lyon on 2 September 1944, the regiment began the Vosges campaign near the German border. They fought a terrible battle near Weyerscheim with the Germans in January 1945, with the 2nd Battalion taking the brunt of the attack. The last great battle of the war for the regiment was the effort to breach the Siegfried Line and reach the Rhine River, missions which were accomplished.

With the rest of the 36th Division, they were turned southeast in the Danube Plain, following the 10th Armored Division, with the 141st capturing Bad Toelz, May 1, 1945. The 143rd Infantry suffered 9,000 casualties, captured 75,000 German Army prisoners, and five Medals of Honor were presented to members of the unit and five Presidential Unit Citations were awarded for units of the Regiment. They served for 386 days in combat.

Deactivation: The Regiment returned to the United States on December 22, 1945 and was inactivated at Camp Patrick Henry, Virginia on that date. They were "home for Christmas."

WORLD WAR II CAMPAIGNS: Naples-Foggia, Anzio, Rome-Arno, Southern France, Rhineland, Ardennes-Alsace, Central Europe.

POST WORLD WAR II: The 143rd Infantry Regiment was reactivated as a component of the 36th Infantry Division, Texas National Guard, on 23 October 1946, with three battalions generally located in the eastern and southeastern regions of the State.
1959 — The Pentomic Infantry Division: On 16 March 1959, during the Pentomic Army restructuring of the national military forces, elements of the of the 143rd were organized as components of the First and Second Battle Groups, 143rd Combat Arms Regiment. During these years, the three separate infantry battalions of the 143rd were deactivated.

1 March 1963: Units of the 143rd Infantry were reorganized from the Pentomic concept to the traditional infantry division structure, with 2nd and 3rd Battalions of the 143rd assigned to the 3rd Brigade, 36th Division. The 1st Battalion was not reactivated.

1 November, 1965: The 3/143rd was relieved of assignment to the 36th Infantry Division and assigned to the 36th Infantry Brigade (Sep) .

30 July 1968: With the retirement of the 36th Infantry Division in 1968, the 1/143rd was reactivated, the 2/143rd was relieved of assignment to the 36th Infantry Division and 3/143rd was reassigned from the 36th Infantry Brigade (Sep). All were assigned to the 71st Infantry Brigade (Airborne). The Brigade also included 1/133rd Artillery, 371st Support Bn., 271st Engineer Company and Troop A, 124th Armored Cavalry.

1973: In 1973, the 71st Infantry Brigade (Airborne) was reorganized as the 36th Infantry Brigade (Airborne) at the same time as the reactivation of the 49th Armored Division. The 1/143rd and 2/143rd were retained as the troop units of the 36th Brigade. Redesignated as the 1st Squadron, 124th Armored Cavalry, the 3/143rd was retired from the Texas National Guard.

Current Unit Assignments: Company G/2/143rd remains as an airborne Long Range Recon and Patrol unit, with elements in Houston and Austin. No other active National Guard units wear the crest of the 143rd Infantry Regiment.

LINEAGE OF SUBORDINATE UNITS. Many units of the 143rd have unit ties which trace back to the War Between the States, the post-war Volunteer Militia Companies, and the Spanish American War.

Company A of Rusk has a lineage which includes Company A, Seventh Confederate Cavalry (Civil War); a militia company at Rusk, 1883-1895, Company F, Third Texas, 1903-1914. It exchanged unit designation with a neighboring unit at Alto, Texas, in 1924, and retained the Company A designation through World War II and the post war reorganization. The unit is entitled to the "ALSACE" Distinguished Unit Streamer.

Company B has a lineage at Mexia, Texas, since 1928, but earlier units connected to its heritage included Company B, Third Infantry, Texas Volunteer Guard, in 1879. It served as Company C, Second Texas, USV, in the Spanish American War. It did border service in 1916-1915. ALSACE STREAMER.

Company C of Beaumont was organized on November 24, 1926 and was mobilized for World War on November 25, 1940. It served as a unit of the 143rd in World War II and was stationed at Palestine after reorganization of the 143rd in 1947. ALSACE STREAMER.

Company D traces lineage to 1859, when Captain John Henry Brown organized a militia unit known as the "Independent Blues." The unit was used to ward off Indian raids of the time. It became Company K, First Texas Cavalry, serving in Louisiana and Arkansas during the War Between the States. It was Company A, First Texas Volunteers in the Spanish American War. ALSACE STREAMER.

Company E was originally organized at Caldwell in 1939 and was federalized on November 25, 1940. The company was an assault unit at Salerno and was decimated by a German armored counterattack. Almost all of the company was killed or captured. Reorganized, the unit was again in the assault at the Rapido River in 1944, holding their ground on the far shore of the river until they ran out of ammunition. After the southern France invasion of 1944, the unit fought northward and was involved in the bloody fighting at the Colmar Pocket in 1945. The unit paid a terrific toll of casualties in those actions. Reorganized in Baytown in 1947. COLMAR POCKET streamer.

Company F of Huntsville traces ancestry to volunteers in Hood's Brigade in the War between the States and the "Tom Hamilton Guards" of the 1870s. That unit was the only Texas unit which were 100% in volunteering for service in the Spanish American War. After the Spanish American war, the Third Texas National Guard regiment was formed from the returning 1st Texas U. S. Volunteers. COLMAR POCKET Distinguished Unit Streamer.

Company G of Houston descended from the "Houston Light Guard Company of 1873." Traditions of that unit still include the wearing of the 19th Century uniforms of the "Light Guard" on ceremonial occasions. COLMAR POCKET Distinguished Unit Streamer.

Company I traces lineage as the Tom Campbell Rifles, organized in 1893.

Company K was organized as the Waco Greys in 1876 and was later redesignated as Company K of the 2nd Texas Infantry in 1898.

Company L was originally organized as Company M of the 2nd Texas infantry in 1900.

Insignia of the
36th Infantry Division

The 36th Infantry Division, the "Texas" division, was raised from National Guard units from Texas and Oklahoma during World War I. The "T" in the division's insignia represents Texas, the arrowhead Oklahoma. The division was also sometimes called the "Lone Star" Division, again symbolizing its Texas roots.

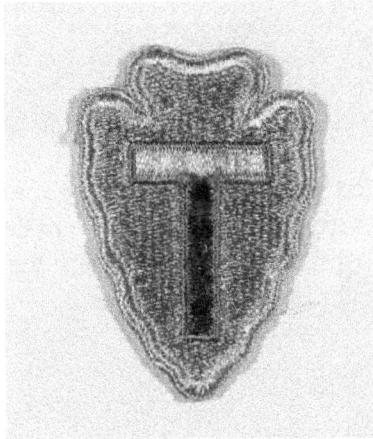

Monument dedicated to 143rd Infantry Regiment, located in Houston. Monument is topped by the T-Patch. In center is the Insignia for 143rd Infantry Regiment. The monument for the 141st Regiment is located in downtown San Antonio, Texas.

Albert DeFazio with daughter Valerie DeFazio Vacula.

Albert DeFazio of Pittsburgh, Pennsylvania, is a World War II veteran of Italian descent. He and his late wife Freda are parents of two children, Valerie and Albert, and grandparents of four, Kristen, Anthony, Nicholas and Natalie, and great-grandparents to Braden and Nico.

Albert worked for the Oakmont Water Company for most of his life after returning home from the war. He began as a meter reader and at times would be called out to help fix a water main break during the winter months. Later he worked in the shop repairing the meters until his retirement at the age of sixty-two.

He loved listening to music and at times would play around on his accordion for amusement. He spent 27 years as the director of his own marching corps known as the Stars and Stripes.

He did what he could for the kids in the neighborhood, often taking them to the water company to show them around, or wrestling with the boys in his front yard. Today he can often be found sitting on his front porch, weather permitting, waving to all who know him.

Valerie DeFazio Vacula is Albert's daughter. Valerie became a majorette in her father's corps at age eleven. Later she became the majorette instructor. When she turned eighteen, she joined a Drum and Bugle Corps, and the color guard became her life until she turned 36 years old.

While in high school she attended cosmetology classes. She took her state boards right after graduation at age 17, and within a few months she was a licensed hairstylist, which has been her job for 41 years. She now has a partnership in her own salon called Sensible Styles located in Verona, Pennsylvania, in the area she grew up.

She has one daughter, Kristen, and one grandson Braden. She met her husband, Keith, online and moved to the Florida Keys to be with him. They knew it was meant to be after they found out they share the same birth date, November 13th. They were married in Key West in 2007. Keith was also born and raised in Pittsburgh, so they moved back to be close to family but look forward to returning south someday.

Albert DeFazio, Company A, 143rd Infantry Regiment,
36th Infantry Division. Naples, Italy, 1943.

Memorabilia from Albert's military service.

Bronze star, awarded for acts of heroism, acts of merit, or meritorious service in a combat zone.

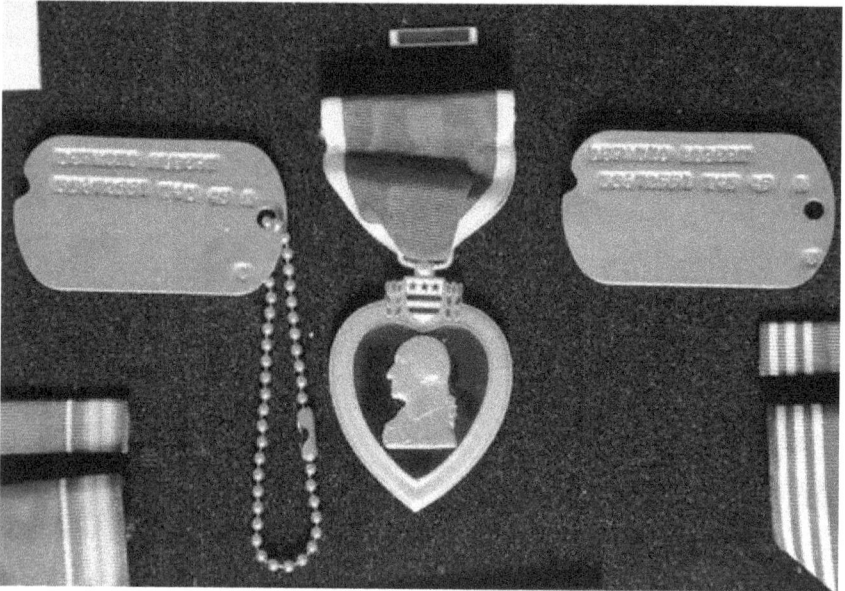

Purple heart, awarded by the President
for being wounded while serving.

World War II Victory Medal and Monte Cassino ring
(reads "1944 Cassino"). This ring and the Anzio ring
were made by an Italian prisoner of war in Algiers,
Africa. When Albert spoke with the prisoner in
Italian, he showed Albert the rings. Albert bought
them off the man for a few dollars.

Two Army Good Conduct Medals awarded for exemplary
behavior, efficiency, and fidelity in active Federal Military service,
a Fifth Army Commemorative medal, and an Anzio ring.

Basic training, Camp Shelby, Mississippi, 1943.

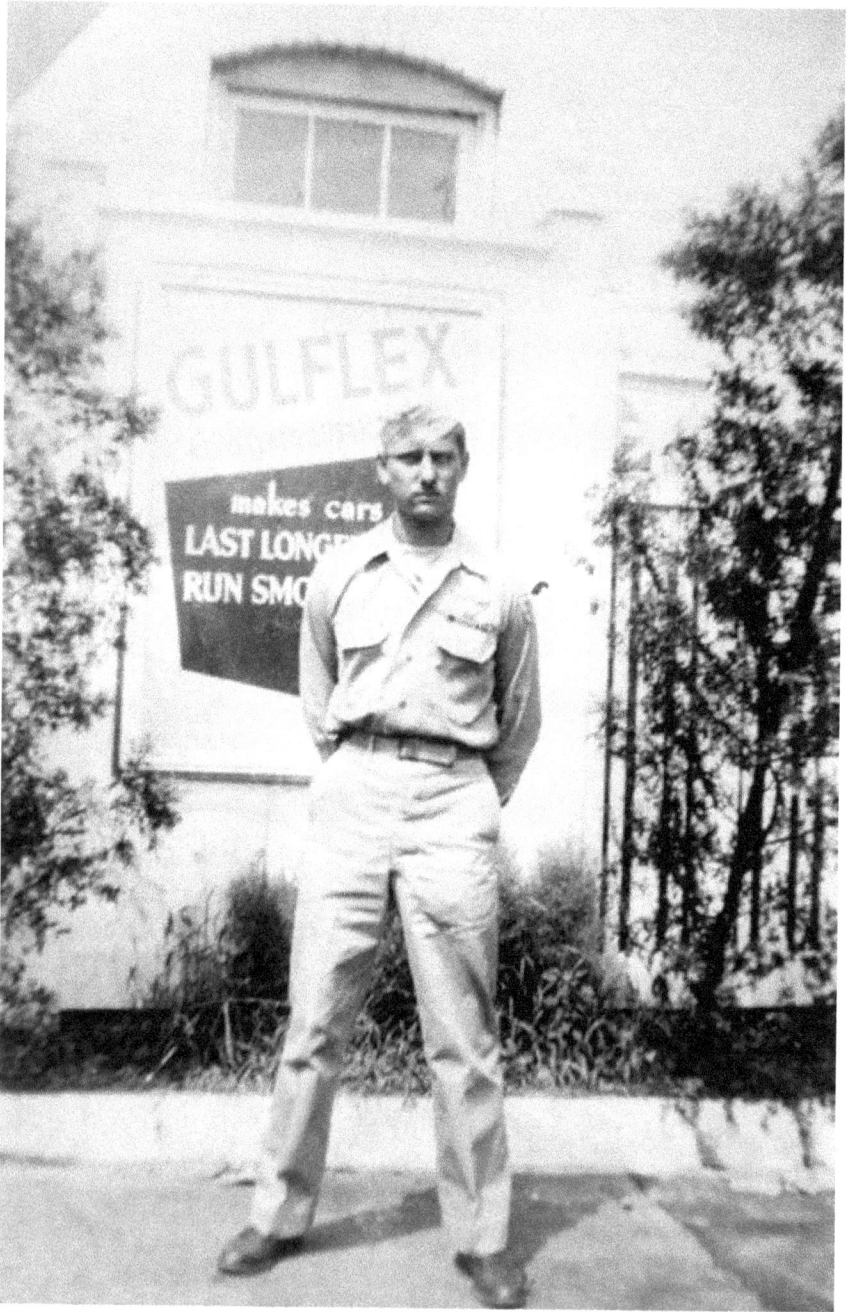

On leave after basic training, before shipping overseas.
Verona, Pennsylvania, 1943.

THE ITALIAN CAMPAIGN

Mount Vesuvius, Pompeii, Italy, 1944.

Passing time at a rest area. Albert is on the right. Caserta, Italy.

Albert on the left. Caserta, Italy.

Albert is on the left. Caserta, Italy.

Algiers, Africa, 1943.

With Tony Arcuri, a friend from basic training. Naples, Italy, 1943.

With a puppy they found. Naples, Italy, 1943.

Albert's brother, William DeFazio, born 1923.
71st Air Group, USAF, postwar.

Albert's brother, Pat DeFazio, born 1924.
28th Infantry Division, U.S. Army.

Albert's brother, Anthony DeFazio, born 1933.
U.S. Navy, USS *Corregidor,* postwar.

American troops in a British LCA (Landing Craft
Assault) which had three benches for seating troops.

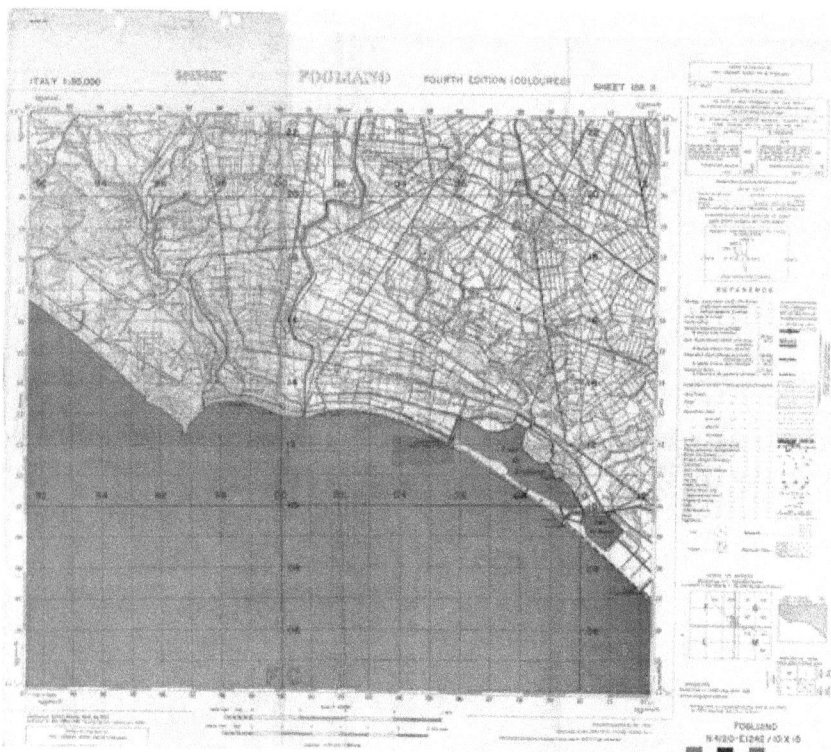

Military Reference Map of Fogliano.

Military Reference Map of Ardea.

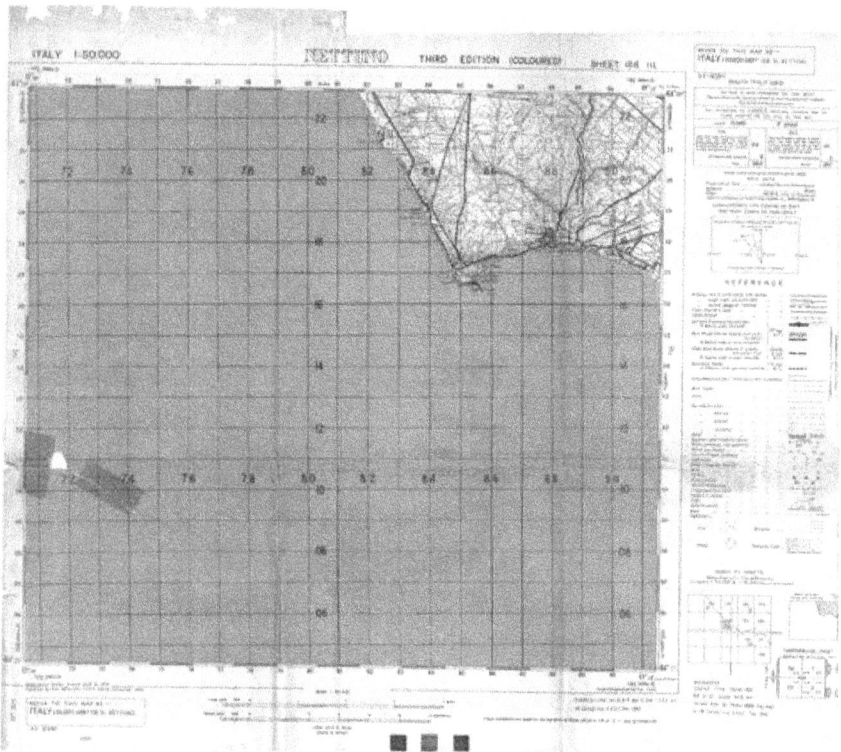

Military Reference Map of Nettuno and Anzio.

Albert and Freda DeFazio's wedding, September 25, 1954.

DeFazio family, April 16, 1958.

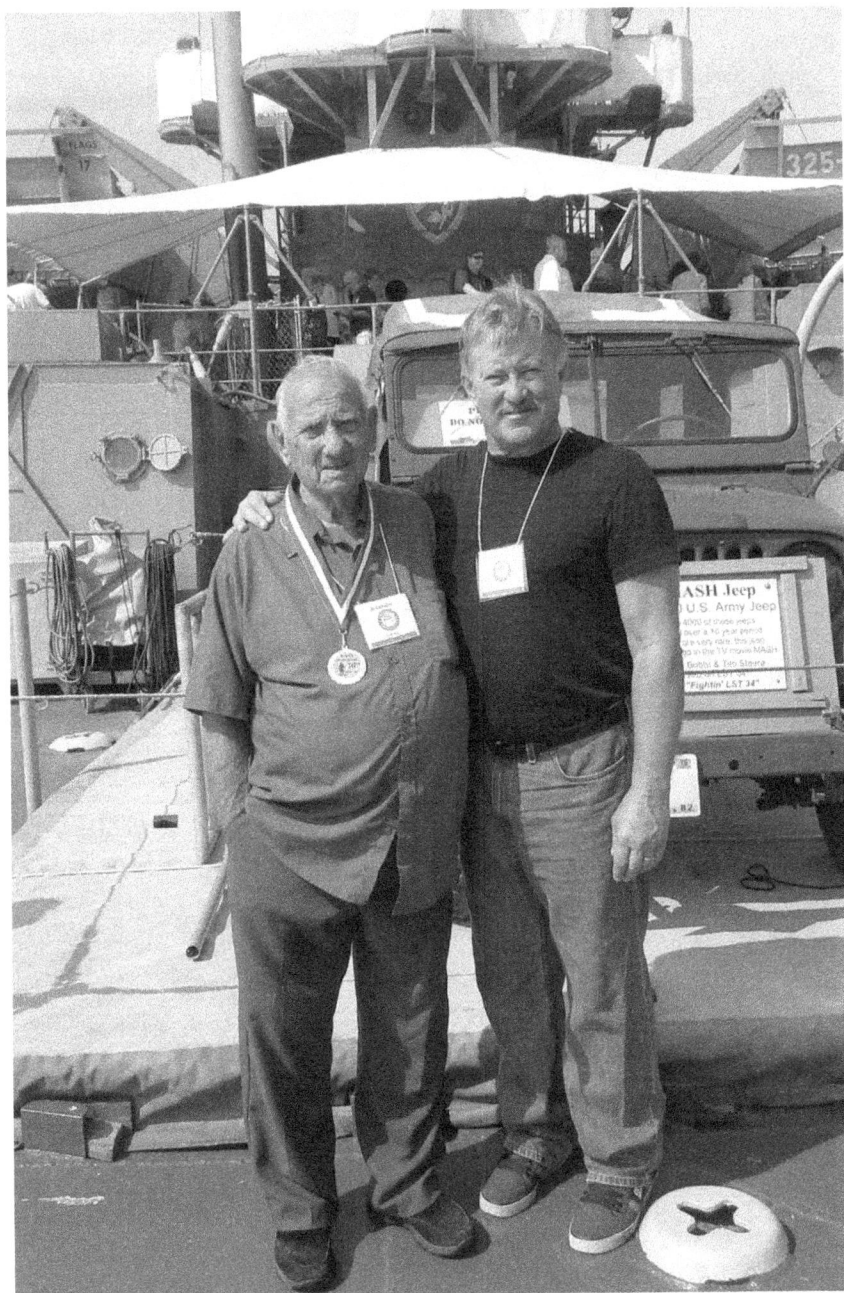

Albert DeFazio and son-in-law Keith Vacula,
also an Army veteran, on the deck of the LST-325
while docked at Pittsburgh on September 4, 2015.

The bow of the restored LST-325 docked at Pittsburgh for a tour, 4 September 2015. This is the same type of ship that Albert was on.

The stern of the restored LST-325
docked at Pittsburgh for a tour, 4 September 2015.

40mm anti-aircraft gun on the deck of the LST-325
while docked at Pittsburgh, September 4, 2015.

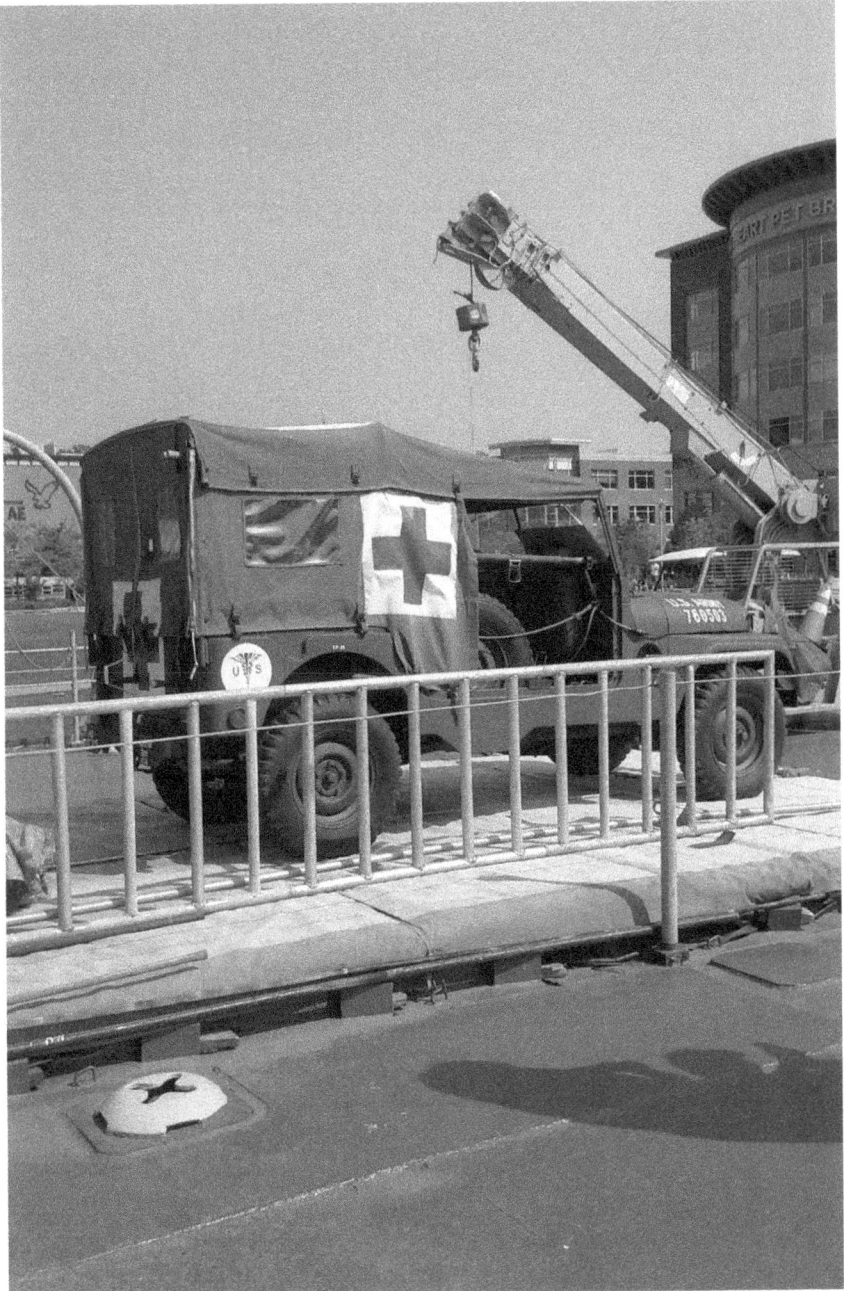

Korean War era ambulance jeep on the deck of
the LST-325 while docked at Pittsburgh, September 4, 2015.

Albert DeFazio.

Scenes from a Forgotten War

Naples and its famous bay, with Vesuvius in the background.
Captured on October 1, 1943, the city for Allied soldiers soon became "the nearest symbol of every man's immediate aspirations,"
one British officer wrote, "a fairyland of silver and gold." Salerno
Bay lay south across the Sorrento Peninsula, seen in the upper
right.

THE ITALIAN CAMPAIGN

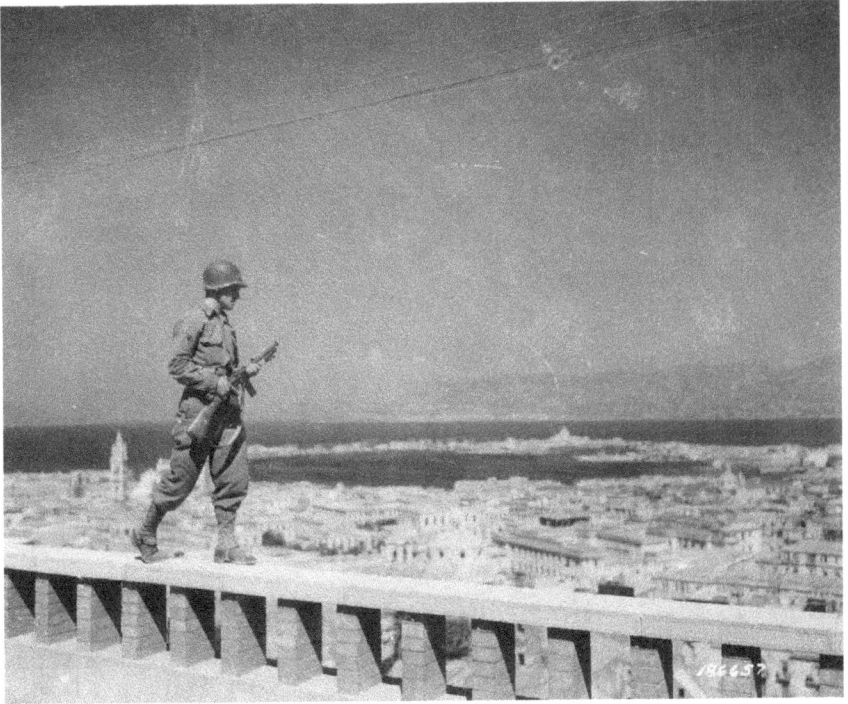

A GI walks guard duty above the city of Naples.

Fifth Army soldiers lined up outside the San Carlo Opera House
in Naples to see "This Is the Army," a musical comedy by Irving
Berlin.

Soldiers try to extract a truck from the mud in central Italy in the fall of 1943.

Italian women washing clothes in a village trough in central Italy as an Allied convoy crawls through mud that seemed to grow thicker and deeper by the day.

Fifth Army engineers finish a bridge across a streambed in central Italy to replace the span destroyed by German demolitionists. In 20 months of fighting in Italy, the Allies would erect 3,000 spans, with a combined length of 55 miles. This one took ten hours to build.

San Pietro reduced to ruins, December 1943. The eviscerated church of St. Michael the Archangel can be seen looming over other buildings in the village.

U.S. troops from the 504th Airborne Infantry Regiment and 143rd Infantry climb through the rubble of San Pietro on December 17, 1943. A gunner described the village as "one large mound of desolation."

Medics from the 36th Infantry Division move into San Pietro, December 1943.

The bodies of U.S. soldiers killed on Christmas Day 1943 are collected in San Pietro before being hauled by truck to a temporary cemetery.

Lieutenant General Mark W. Clark.

Once described as an "amiable mastiff," Major General Fred L. Walker had been Mark Clark's instructor at the Army War College in the 1930s. As the Rapido attack turned into a debacle, Walker's disaffection increased. "The stupidity of some higher commanders seems to be profound," he wrote.

From Monte Trocchio, the view north across the Rapido River to Sant' Angelo and the Liri Valley beyond, January 1944.

Mud and the 36th Division Supply Dump, Mignano Area.

Smoke pots burning at the Rapido.

THE ITALIAN CAMPAIGN

Infantrymen of the 36th Division move out across the mine-littered approach to the Rapido River.

Soldiers removing a German mine in central Italy, January 1944.

THE ITALIAN CAMPAIGN

Major General Geoffrey Keyes, commander of the U.S. II Corps,
next to a M4 medium tank near the front on January 22, 1944, the
day of the Rapido River attack.

Infantrymen from the 143rd Infantry, 36th Division, take refuge from sniper and mortar fire near the Rapido River on January 22, 1944.

THE ITALIAN CAMPAIGN

Mortar crewmen drop another round down the tube near the Rapido River on January 24, 1944. Before the attack, the 36th Division commander, Major General Fred L. Walker, had scribbled in his diary, "We are undertaking the impossible, but I shall keep it to myself."

Two signalmen use a pig sty as a message center during the battle for the Rapido, January 23, 1944. A censor has marked through the sign indicating that the men belong to the 143rd Infantry Regiment of the 36th Division. Observed one sergeant, "Anybody who had any experience knew this ain't the place to cross the river."

THE ITALIAN CAMPAIGN

Medics of the 36th Infantry Division, Texas National Guard, carry
a wounded GI to an aid station right behind the lines at the
Rapido River, near Monte Cassino, Italy on January 24, 1944.

Bogged-down American Medium Tank M4 near the Rapido.

American soldiers near Naples stage for the assault on Anzio,
January 1944.

Anzio was the birthplace of two notorious Roman emperors, Nero and Caligula. Her sister city, Nettuno, can be seen down the coastline (center right), just beyond the dark patch of the Borghese estate; the seventeenth-century villa commandeered by Mark Clark as a Fifth Army command post is also visible in the center of the estate. Beyond the coast, the Pontine Marshes stretch to the distant hills.

Men and equipment move ashore south of Anzio on D-day.

A U.S. Sherman tank crosses the dunes near Nettuno, January 1944.

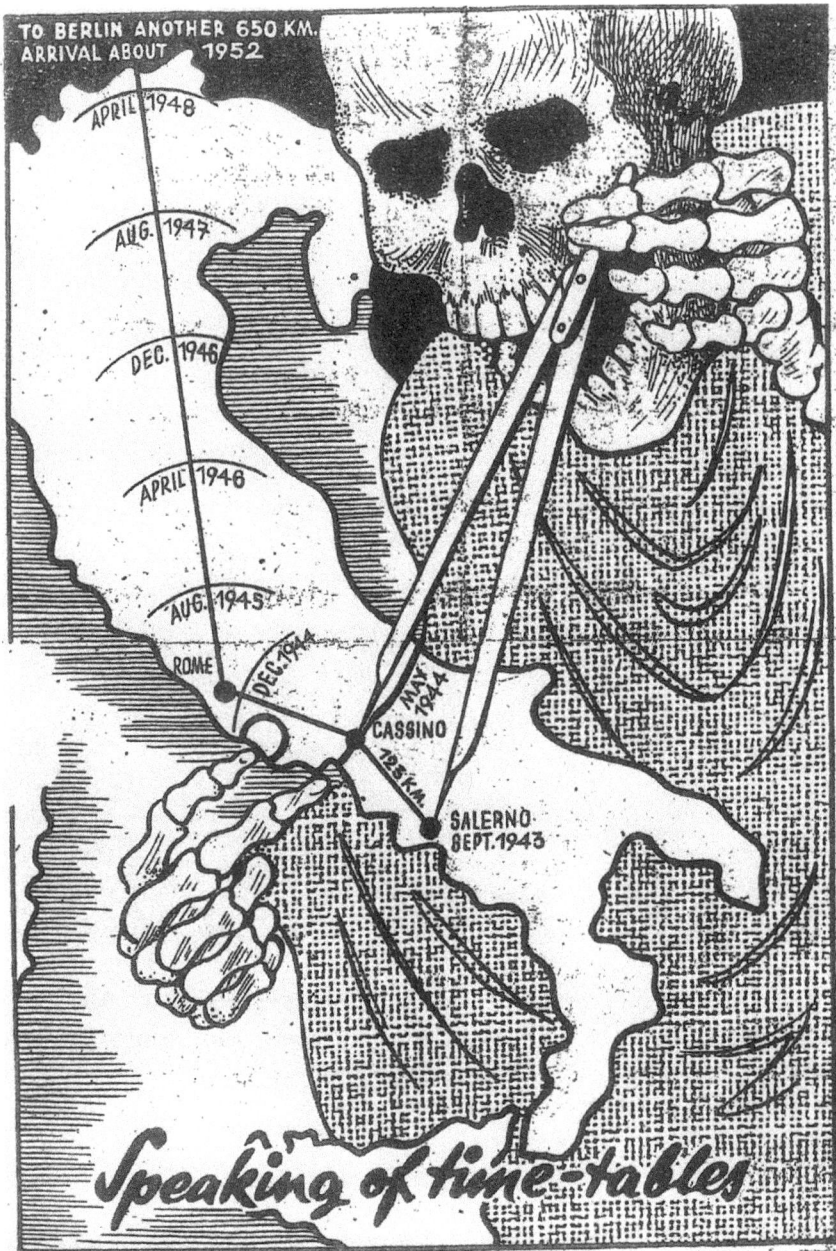

A German propaganda leaflet at Cassino, depicting the slow pace
of the Allied advance in Italy.

American soldiers in the Rapido valley on February 6, 1944, eye the abbey atop Monte Cassino, with snow-capped Monte Cairo in the background.

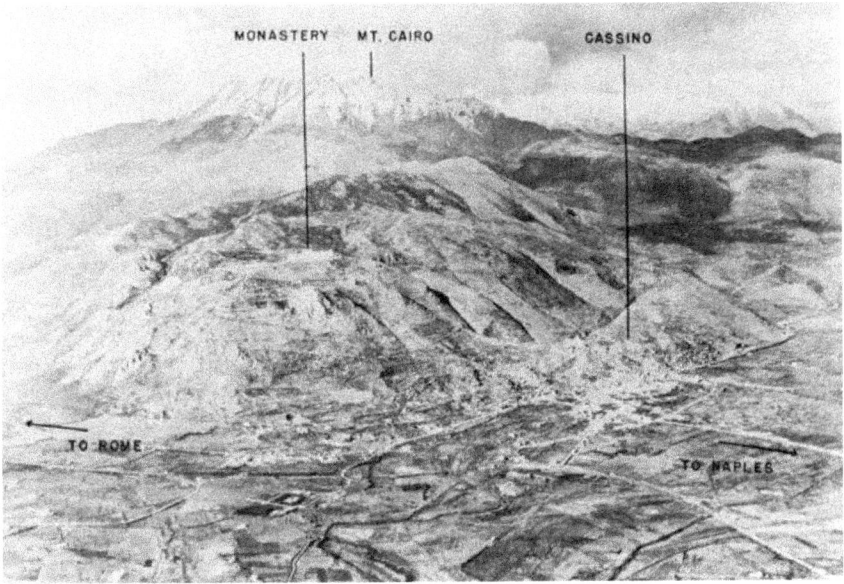

The Cassino Area.

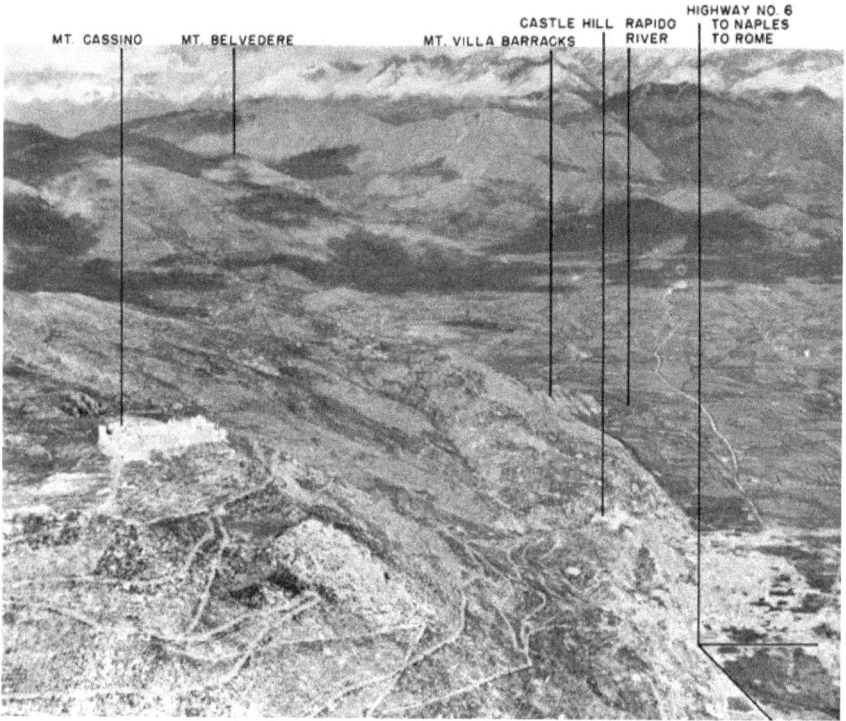

The ruins of Monte Cassino abbey, with the Via Serpentina
leading up from Cassino town.

THE ITALIAN CAMPAIGN

Artillery fire rakes Castle Hill above Cassino town on February 6, 1944. The famous Benedictine abbey looming on Monte Cassino would survive another nine days before Allied bombers pulverized the building.

U.S. Army military policemen toasting bread over molten lava from Vesuvius. The volcano's spectacular eruption, which began on March 18, 1944, would be the last of the twentieth century.

Living conditions at the front diving the latter part of the Anzio campaign were much improved as the men protected their fox holes with sandbags, tarpauline, and camouflaged roofs. Fighting was light and living was leisurely, disturbed only by sporadic shelling and bombing.

In Hell's Half Acre at Anzio, troops in early April 1944 dig in another hospital tent against German artillery and air attacks. In a single episode two months earlier, a Luftwaffe pilot jettisoned his bombs during a dogfight over the beachhead and the blasts killed 28 people — including three nurses, two doctors, and six patients.

Tanks from the 1st Armored Division roll from an LST in Anzio harbor on April 27, 1944, among the reinforcements preparing to blast out of the beachhead after four months' confinement.

Pfc. Edward J. Foley of Methuen, Massachusetts, an American sniper with the 143rd Infantry Regiment, 36th Infantry Division, gives his M1903A4 sniper rifle a thorough check before heading to the front during the Italian Campaign. Velletri, Province of Rome, Lazio, Italy. May 20, 1944.

1st Armored Division tanks pushing from the Anzio beachhead on May 30, 1944.

Postscript

Thanks to social media I have been able to connect with family members of the 36th Infantry Division. After posting some information about my dad on pages that I follow, I received this message:

> Dear Ms. Vacula,
> My grandfather was the Captain of the 143rd, A Company, can you tell me what regiment and company was your father in?
> Matthew Henry

I messaged him back letting him know my father was in the same unit. After a few conversations and sharing his grandfather's picture, I was able to show my father this information, and low and behold, Captain Daniel Lee Henry, who served as captain from April 1944 until June 1944 was the same captain my dad shared those cigars with and gave him his two-day leave to visit family.

Matthew's grandfather is now gone but would be proud to know that Matthew keeps learning everything he can to keep Captain Henry's legacy alive.

www.ingramcontent.com/pod-product-compliance
Lightning Source LLC
Chambersburg PA
CBHW020514100426

42813CB00030B/3236/J